Timeless Wisdom for the New Millennium

Well over two millennia have passed since Sun Tzu wrote *The Art of War*. Although the rate of change has accelerated in each millennium, the timeless wisdom of the strategic rules set forth by Sun Tzu has not changed. Fundamental strategic truths are the same for all times and all generations.

The objective of this book is to make Sun Tzu's simple and timeless strategies useful to managers in the new millennium. Your success using ideas from this book is my success. My wish is that this new translation and analysis will contribute to your continued success.

—*Gerald A. Michaelson*

Worldwide Praise for *Sun Tzu: The Art of War for Managers*

"The Michaelson name is the 'true north' for practical and useful tools for those who manage people and process. Building on the legacy of his father's work, Steve Michaelson once again leverages the ancient and timeless teachings of Sun Tzu into the manager's field manual for success. Whether you carry a backpack, a briefcase, or a Kindle, this book is a must."

—*Mark Davidoff*, Partner, Deloitte Financial Advisory Services

"Sun Tzu's writings, and Michaelson's interpretation of the logical thought processes therein, are an unsurpassed management tool for anyone seeking to improve the quality of their decision-making."

—*Gerry Hodes*, Executive Head of Marketing & Selling Management, Marks & Spencer Food Division, London, UK

"The new millennium is where East meets West. This book reveals creative applications of Sun Tzu's strategic wisdom in management."

—*Frank L. Hung*, Chairman, Harvard Management Services, Inc., Taipei, Taiwan

"As global competition approaches the intensity of war, *Sun Tzu: The Art of War for Managers* is a brilliant companion, linking time-honored military concepts to sound business strategy. Don't go into battle without it."

—*Bill Griffiths*, President, Fluid Handling Division, United Dominion Industries, USA

"Sun Tzu's *Art of War* is the definitive work on military strategy. Michaelson's commentary makes The Art of War for Managers the definitive work on business strategy."

—*Roger Eriksson*, ABB Business Academy, Vasteras, Sweden

Sun Tzu

2nd Edition

THE ART of WAR for MANAGERS

50 STRATEGIC RULES
UPDATED FOR TODAY'S BUSINESS

GERALD A. MICHAELSON and STEVEN MICHAELSON

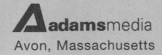
Avon, Massachusetts

To my father, the Business Master I learned from.
—Steven Michaelson

Published by
Adams Media, a division of F+W Media, Inc.
57 Littlefield Street, Avon, MA 02322. U.S.A.
www.adamsmedia.com

ISBN 10: 1-60550-030-5
ISBN 13: 978-1-60550-030-0
eISBN 10: 1-4405-0708-2
eISBN 13: 978-1-4405-0708-3

Printed in the United States of America.

10   9   8   7   6   5   4   3

Library of Congress Cataloging-in-Publication Data
is available from the publisher.

This publication is designed to provide accurate and authoritative information with regard to the subject matter covered. It is sold with the understanding that the publisher is not engaged in rendering legal, accounting, or other professional advice. If legal advice or other expert assistance is required, the services of a competent professional person should be sought.
—From a *Declaration of Principles* jointly adopted by a Committee of the American Bar Association and a Committee of Publishers and Associations

Many of the designations used by manufacturers and sellers to distinguish their product are claimed as trademarks. Where those designations appear in this book and Adams Media was aware of a trademark claim, the designations have been printed with initial capital letters.

This book is available at quantity discounts for bulk purchases.
For information, please call 1-800-289-0963.

Contents

Part One:
New Translation of *The Art of War*
with Manager's Commentary

Chapter One: Laying Plans / 3

Chapter Two: Waging War / 13

Chapter Three: Attack by Stratagem / 24

Chapter Four: Disposition of Military Strength / 36

Chapter Five: Use of Energy / 45

Chapter Six: Weakness and Strength / 54

Chapter Seven: Maneuvering / 68

Chapter Eight: Variation of Tactics / 82

Part Two:
Applying Sun Tzu's Wisdom

Acknowledgments
for the First Edition

As always, Steven and Deanne provided ideas, while Jan supported my interest in the strange hobby of searching for business applications from military strategy.

With thanks for world-class performance to Erny James, who designed the cover art, and Sandy Belcher, a talented and tireless editor who gets everything right.

Jere Calmes, Jeff Cowell, Carl Glass, Trent Price, Townes Osborn, and Steve Rivkin gave awesome advice concerning major changes in format and content.

My thanks to many friends who offered ideas and input during the eight years of intermittent writing and rewriting of this book. The most recent helpful contributions were offered by Roger Bean, Tim Carpenter, Suzzane Dupes, Tom Gordon, Frank Hung, Irving Mills, Vergil Metts, Allen Pannell, John Shamley, Chuck Sawyer, and Jerry Sentell. My apologies to those I may have missed.

With sincere appreciation to the staff at TAI who cheerfully performed myriad support tasks, including Stephanie Daugherty, Kaye Dennison, Connie Fancher, Felesa Honeycutt, Elaine Lasher, Richard Lebo, Angela Murr, Charlie Norton, Lynda Perkins, Otie Smith, and Lisa Taylor.

Thanks to friends in Beijing: Zhai Zhihai, who introduced me to the new translation; Mr. Chen Yingming, for his gracious assistance in arranging contacts; and Ms. Wu Ying, for making arrangements with Mr. Chen Shufang, who gave approval on behalf of his publishing house to use this translation of *The Art of War*.

Foreword to the Second Edition

Sun Tzu is frequently referred to in writings as "the master" for the concise and enduring wisdom of his book *The Art of War*.

Not quite as enduring, but still highly successful, was my father's original book on Sun Tzu's *The Art of War*, *The Art of War for Managers: 50 Strategic Rules*. Since its publication in 1999, over 100,000 copies have been sold, quite a number for a business book. It has been translated into over a dozen languages, published on audio discs from the United States to Romania, and is now available in various digital forms. My father passed away in 2004. Many business books have come and gone since then, and the number of Sun Tzu business books has multiplied, but the popularity of *The Art of War for Managers* has never waned.

My father did two things (besides being an executive of a major publicly traded company). One, he wrote. He wrote articles, books, and regular columns. He wrote on business, quality assurance, travel, and sales. He wrote and wrote, until he became very good at it. Second, he worked to apply the lessons in military success and failure to business success and failure. In the eighties, he began to develop his thinking and lectured on *Winning the Marketing War* on every continent. He used both Western military thought (from Machiavelli to The Duke of Saxony to Montgomery) and Eastern military thinkers (from Sun Tzu to Mao). Eventually, that culminated in his focus on Eastern military thought as applied to business and in *The Art of War for Managers*.

As in any book using contemporary business examples to illustrate points (and deepen learning), some of the examples, the business stories, have become dated. So the intent of this edition is to update these business examples, add a few more contemporary examples where they help, and by updating these examples better help readers connect the learning from Sun Tzu to their business challenges. During this edit, I worked to stay very true to the structure of the book and simply changed examples where needed. Some stories I replaced, some I updated, but my hand as editor was intentionally a light one. The overall narrative remains strongly its original voice.

Editing this book was another chance for me to dig in to the core writing of Sun Tzu from a foundational business perspective. I have done this from scratch for other books in this series, but an edit is different; you are working to build new connections from original writings.

In Part II, Applying Sun Tzu's Wisdom, many of the stories and voices are new. I hope the more contemporary examples help readers gain a clearer understanding of how Sun Tzu's wisdom applies to the contemporary business world. That was the original role of the business examples.

Sun Tzu's *The Art of War* remains popular in our culture, and the growth of China's economic strength will likely only increase interest in Sun Tzu's writings. On a recent trip there, I learned China had opened a Sun Tzu institute in his birthplace. They have a goal of educating managers, entrepreneurs, and MBA students. Clearly, China is taking a strong natural position on the study of Sun Tzu!

The purpose of this book remains unchanged from its original writing: to help the reader take the timeless advice of Sun Tzu, apply that to business, and make better, winning, business decisions. I wish you every success outmaneuvering your business opponents.

—Steve Michaelson
April 2010

The Lesson of the Concubines

The following story is considered to be of dubious authenticity and not part of the thirteen chapters. Some translators include it within their books; others ignore its existence. All narratives are quite similar. You may find interesting lessons in the following version.

Sun Tzu's book, *The Art of War*, earned him an audience with the King of Wu, who said, "I have thoroughly read your thirteen chapters. May I submit your theory of managing soldiers to a small test?"

Sun Tzu replied, "Sir, you may."

The King of Wu asked, "Can the test be applied to women?"

Sun Tzu replied that it could, so arrangements were made to bring 180 beautiful women from the palace. Sun Tzu divided them into two companies with one of the King's favorite concubines at the head of each. He then made all of them take spears in their hands and spoke to them: "I presume you know the difference between front and back, right hand, and left hand?"

The women replied, "Yes."

Sun Tzu continued, "When to the sound of drums I order 'eyes front,' look straight ahead. When I order 'left turn,' face toward your left hand. When I order 'right turn,' face toward your right hand. When I order 'about turn,' face around to the back."

After the words of command had been explained, the women agreed they understood. He gave them spears so he could begin the drill. To the sound of drums, Sun Tzu ordered "right turn." In response, the women burst out in laughter.

With great patience, Sun Tzu said, "If the instructions and words of command are not clear and distinct, if orders are not thoroughly understood, then the general is to blame." He then repeated the explanations several times. This time he ordered the drums to signal "left turn," and again the women burst into laughter.

Then Sun Tzu said, "If the instructions and words of command are not clear and distinct, if orders are not thoroughly understood, the general is to blame. But if commands are clear and the soldiers disobey, then it is the fault of the officers." He immediately ordered the women who were at the head of the two companies to be beheaded.

Of course, the King was watching from a raised pavilion, and when he saw that his two favorite concubines were about to be executed, he was alarmed and swiftly sent down a message: "We are now quite satisfied as to the general's ability to manage troops. Without these concubines, my food and drink will not taste good. It is the King's wish that they not be beheaded."

Sun Tzu replied, "Having received the sovereign's commission to take charge and direct these troops, there are certain orders I cannot accept." He immediately had the two concubines beheaded as an example and appointed the two next in line as the new leaders.

Now the drums were sounded again and the drill began. The women performed all the maneuvers exactly as commanded, turning to the right or left, marching ahead, turning around, kneeling, or rising. They drilled perfectly in precision and did not utter a single sound.

Sun Tzu sent a messenger to the King of Wu saying, "Your Majesty, the soldiers are now correctly drilled and perfectly disciplined. They are ready for your inspection. Put them to any use you desire. As sovereign, you may choose to require them to go through fire and water and they will not disobey."

The King responded, "Our commander should cease the drill and return to his camp. We do not wish to come down and inspect the troops."

With great calm, Sun Tzu said, "This king is only fond of words and cannot carry them into deeds."

Commentary following the story indicates that the King relented, recognized Sun Tzu's ability, and appointed him a general; and Sun Tzu won many battles. In contrast, some historians believe Sun Tzu simply served as a civilian strategist, and others deny his existence, claiming he was actually someone else.

The moral of the story could be a lesson on training, discipline, command structure, role-play, or perhaps job interviews. The thoughtful reader may use his imagination to determine applicable lessons.

Introduction

As I stood in the Great Hall of the People in Beijing, China, an entourage was approaching. The next thing I knew I was shaking hands with the Premier of China—Li Peng. The personal introduction was part of a journey to China to present applications of Sun Tzu's strategies for business at an international symposium on *The Art of War.* Sun Tzu was a practical philosopher who wrote the 7,000-word *The Art of War* in about 500 B.C. I read it while researching my book *Winning the Marketing War* and found the content quite useful.

If you've read James Clavell's *Noble House* or seen the movie *Wall Street,* you've encountered some of the wisdom of this ancient Chinese strategist. In both the book and the movie, major characters quote from Sun Tzu as a foundation for their strategy.

The Art of War might be one of the oldest books you will ever read. Originally written on bamboo strips, this acclaimed work has achieved international recognition as *the* concentrated essence of winning strategy.

For centuries, *The Art of War* has held a pre-eminent position among both Chinese and Japanese strategists. Many of the sayings of Chairman Mao are simple restatements of Sun Tzu's philosophies.

When Chiang Kai-shek's military attaché advised British military strategist B. H. Liddell Hart that Chinese officers were trained from Hart's books, he replied it was time they went back to Sun Tzu:

> *Since in that one short book was embodied almost as much about the fundamentals of strategy and tactics as I [Hart] had covered in more than twenty books. In brief, Sun Tzu was the best short introduction to the study of warfare.*

Confirming again that *The Art of War* is *the* sound fundamental text on strategy.

EASTERN VERSUS WESTERN STRATEGY

The Art of War is the foundation of Eastern strategy. Sun Tzu's central thesis is that you can avoid fighting when you plan the right strategy before the battle. *On War* by Carl von Clausewitz, a German officer who wrote in Napoleon's time, is the foundation of much of Western strategy. Clausewitzian theory concentrates on the big battle as the way to win.

Readers will find *On War* filled with convoluted sentences and difficult to read. One English translation is over 600 pages long. Clausewitz's work expresses so many ideas that it can be used to justify any position. In contrast, *The Art of War* is a masterpiece of simplicity. When comparing Clausewitz and Sun Tzu, strategist Liddell Hart comments: "Sun Tzu has clearer vision, more profound insight, and eternal freshness." Although there is evidence that a translation of *The Art of War* could have been available to Napoleon, Sun Tzu's work has not generally been considered to contribute to Western military strategy.

Locked within Sun Tzu are secrets for business and personal success. Continued study and analysis of Sun Tzu yields new insights to unlock winning concepts.

A STRATEGIC MANUAL FOR BUSINESS LEADERS

Using Sun Tzu's strategies in business is nothing new. The existence of over 100 Japanese translations of *The Art of War* indicates it has served as a source of strategic thinking for many Japanese managers. In contrast, only a handful of English translations exist, but they are circulated throughout the business world.

There is much evidence that *The Art of War* is making significant contributions to the thinking of contemporary business leaders. Harvard Professor Michael Porter quoted from Sun Tzu when he lectured the National Football League owners on how they could defeat the now-defunct United States Football League. Venture capitalist Asher Edelman made *The Art of War* required reading for admission to his course on entrepreneurship at Columbia University. Quantity orders for *The Art of War* have been placed by business organizations, trade unions, and law-enforcement agencies. Western officers who laid plans for the first Gulf War were well versed in Sun Tzu; it would seem as though Saddam Hussein was not.

The Art of War is a classic not only of strategy but also of simplicity. There was nothing very complex about warfare in Sun Tzu's time. It involved land battles of large bodies of troops armed with personal weapons. The simplicity of *The Art of War* makes Sun Tzu's lessons readily transferable to business strategy and understanding the strategic rules of business in the new millennium.

The lessons of Sun Tzu are thousands of years old, and it is the test of time that makes the ancient lessons valuable to the business manager. Many business lessons have existed for such a short time that they have yet to crystallize as valid strategies. Evidence of respect for the passage of time to give veracity to lessons comes from a Chinese historian asked in 1925 to identify the lessons of the French Revolution. He replied, "I would love to, but it is still too early to tell."

STRATEGY AND TACTICS

The fundamental principles of strategy are the same for all managers, all times, and all situations. Only the tactics change, and tactics are modified to the times.

Strategy is best defined as "doing the right thing," while tactics is "doing things right." Where does strategy end and tactics begin? Admiral Mahan in his work on sea power said, "Contact is a word which perhaps better than any other indicates the dividing line between tactics and strategy." Strategy stops at the border in war and at the headquarters door in business; tactics begins with contact with the enemy in war and at the customer in business. Sun Tzu's *The Art of War* provides fundamental lessons for contemporary strategic thought and serves as a fertile source of ideas for tactics.

ABOUT THIS EDITION

Because there are so few English language translations of *The Art of War,* the emergence of a new translation has special significance. I felt fortunate indeed when I received this translation in Beijing at a symposium sponsored by The Research Society of Sun Tzu's *The Art of War.* Translation of Chinese ideograms into English is a complex task because each character can have many different meanings. Consequently, the personal and professional backgrounds of the translators tend to determine the wording of the translation. The Chinese language scholars who undertook the difficult task of translating from the original documents concentrated on finding the most accurate interpretations of the ideograms.

As author, I made an exhaustive search to locate all English-language translations. Each translation has been reviewed to find areas where different interpretations would benefit the reader. These alternate translations are used throughout the text to clarify Sun Tzu's wisdom.

Eastern and Western strategic writings exist as two distinct and separate sources of information, seldom communicating with each other. Western strategists build upon the strengths of previous Western strategists; Eastern strategists similarly reinforce each other. Neither builds on the strength of the other. An important contribution of this work is to provide a conceptual linkage between the fundamental lessons of the two. By analyzing key concepts from both Eastern and Western strategic thought, you gain an insight into how *both* can strengthen your strategy *and* tactics.

This book does not propose a short list of key strategies, but rather is formulated around the understanding that strategy is a mental process. The best strategy comes from the right mindset. Clausewitz said, "Theory can give no formula with which to solve problems. It lets the mind take a look at objects and their relations and then the mind goes to higher regions of action, there to act." *Sun Tzu: The Art of War for Managers* provides a refreshing way to immerse oneself in the great strategic thinking which nurtures the mind.

This new translation of Sun Tzu is a joy to read—and read again. Sun Tzu's lessons can be applied to real-life situations and serve as an everyday resource for all kinds of strategic thought. For example, one version of *The Art of War* relates Sun Tzu's principles to winning in the stock market. An English translation, *The Art of Strategy,* is organized as a template for the strategies of life.

The strategic lessons in *The Art of War* have become a general construct to solve a variety of problems. Although the original text is founded in military strategy, the applications in this book focus on strategic issues for managers.

READER'S GUIDE

Like the original work, Part I is divided into thirteen chapters. Unlike the original work, each chapter is subdivided into three to six discrete strategic rules.

Each chapter has the same title as the original translation. The first page lists the strategic rules in that chapter followed by a brief commentary. Opposite each page of Sun Tzu's translation is business commentary on that strategic rule.

Because the flow of the book faithfully maintains the sequential order of Sun Tzu's translation, there is no modern strategic construct. Rather, each strategic rule stands alone as an idea generator for the contemporary strategist.

Because the content of the book flows from Sun Tzu's philosophy, it should not be considered a complete modern strategic manual. Instead, the value of this book is its ability to simplify the complexity of strategic thinking. While you may want to take the strategic wisdom of Sun Tzu seriously, do not take the modern translation of the ancient words too literally.

—*Gerald A. Michaelson*
March 1999

PART ONE

New Translation of
THE ART OF WAR
with Manager's Commentary

Reflecting on Sun Tzu's work is to the business manager what weightlifting is to the champion athlete—an exercise that makes one stronger.

John Kohut
Beijing Bureau Chief
South China Post

Chapter 1

Laying Plans

Strategic Rules

- ▧ Thoroughly Assess Conditions
- ▧ Compare Attributes
- ▧ Look for Strategic Turns

The vision of what the organization wants to be must be planned with an awareness of reality. That is why this chapter focuses on assessment.

The vision components articulate purpose, mission, guiding values, and a vivid image of the organization's future. From the vision, leaders can determine the strategy, set strategic initiatives, and align the organization.

The more sophisticated the planning process becomes, the harder it is to introduce the flexibility to accommodate changes in the situation. In rigid systems, planning and obedience to the plan are regarded as the key to victory. Carefully laid plans rigorously implemented without deviation are regarded as the way to overcome the inevitable confusion. As ever-increasing time and attention are focused on "the process of planning," the successful execution of the plan can become secondary. However, any football coach can tell you that rigidity does not win games. Every coach has plans that allow for flexibility in formations to adapt to reality. It follows that it is not strategists who cause changes in the plan—it is reality.

A common mistake is to consider planning as only a mental process, an idea in our head that simply looks at the past and adjusts for the future. If your plan is not in writing, you do not have a plan at all. Instead, you have only a dream, a vision, or perhaps even a nightmare. The simple written plan works best.

Clearly define the problem before seeking a solution. Do not limit your planning horizon to what can be accomplished with existing tools. If the only tool you have is a hammer, everything will look like a nail.

THOROUGHLY ASSESS CONDITIONS—TRANSLATION

Sun Tzu says:

War is a matter of vital importance to the state; a matter of life and death, the road either to survival or to ruin. Hence, it is imperative that it be thoroughly studied.

Therefore, to make assessment of the outcome of a war, one must compare the various conditions of the antagonistic sides in terms of the five constant factors:*

1. Moral influence
2. Weather
3. Terrain
4. Commander
5. Doctrine

These five constant factors should be familiar to every general. He who masters them wins; he who does not is defeated.

*Business Parallels to Five Constant Factors

1. **Moral influence means a "spirit of mission."** The strength of belief that the purpose is morally sound rallies a fighting spirit and generates a firestorm of commitment.
2. **Weather equates to "outside forces."** The surge of consolidation that is sweeping through every industry is an outside force, as is the emergence of world competition and the influence of environmentalism.
3. **Terrain is the "marketplace."** As the general must know the terrain, so the strategist must consider the scene of action—people, place, product, promotion, price, etc.
4. **Commander has an equivalent in "leadership."** The names keep changing, but the principles of leadership remain the same.
5. **Doctrine is comparable to "guiding principles."** Understand and apply the fundamental principles that determine success.

THOROUGHLY ASSESS CONDITIONS— MANAGER'S COMMENTARY

Good assessment is the foundation of a successful operation.

When the management of a major pharmaceutical company found that product development activity was decreasing, an assessment revealed the reason. Although senior managers claimed development was a team effort, analysis of their twenty-five most profitable drugs revealed that two people initiated ten of them. The reason product development declined was because both people had moved to positions where they were no longer in the development stream.[1]

Every assessment must include a thorough analysis of how to increase business with existing customers. As proof, an Ogilvy & Mather analysis showed that the return on the marketing investment to existing customers can be many times greater than to prospective customers. The greatest source of increased sales and profits is from those who know you and are already purchasing your products.

In today's business world, the assessment before the plan is often ignored in the rush to action. When action is taken without a thorough assessment of the situation, too often people begin working on the wrong things. In these circumstances, the result will be a lot of effort expended with no gain.

Assessments are simply methodologies for gathering data in a structured process designed to elicit facts or perceptions. Assessments can be internal or external and they can be conducted by one or more individuals. Assessments can be surveys distributed to everyone or interviews conducted across a vertical slice of the organization.

Good assessments go beyond the current situation. They dig into underlying causes and search for new and better ways to achieve success. To achieve good results, ask questions in pairs so the first question determines the perception of the current status and the second reveals opportunities. For example, the first question might ask for a definition of an objective, while the second would ask for ideas about how the objective should be achieved.

When assessments are conducted by an external organization, respondents usually feel they have a better chance of giving anonymous input, which provides more accurate data. Internally, the assessment provides information on strengths and weaknesses that can energize and direct self-renewal. Externally, the assessment reveals threats and opportunities.

COMPARE ATTRIBUTES—TRANSLATION

Sun Tzu continues:

Therefore, to forecast the outcome of a war the attributes of the antagonistic sides should be analyzed by* making the following seven comparisons:

1. Which sovereign possesses greater moral influence?
2. Which commander is more capable?
3. Which side holds more favorable conditions in weather and terrain?
4. On which side are decrees better implemented?
5. Which side is superior in arms?
6. On which side are officers and men better trained?
7. Which side is stricter and more impartial in meting out rewards and punishments?

By means of these seven elements, I can forecast victory or defeat.

If the sovereign heeds these stratagems of mine and acts upon them, he will surely win the war, and I shall, therefore, stay with him. If the sovereign neither heeds nor acts upon them, he will certainly suffer defeat, and I shall leave.

*We must compare ourselves with our foe.
—A. L. Sadler

A Strategic Moral

Following the success of the Prussian army in the Franco-Prussian War, the British General Staff sent a team of aristocrats to find out the secret of success. They reported the Prussian troops were all clean-shaven with short-cropped hair. The British Army copied this; it remains a law to this day.

The moral of the story is: Don't copy the wrong thing! (Or, don't send aristocrats to do competitive studies.)

COMPARE ATTRIBUTES—MANAGER'S COMMENTARY

Compare competitive strengths and weaknesses.

When Coke and Pepsi engage in competitive battles, or when P&G determines how to increase market share, these organizations use competitive marketing research as an input ingredient. When Xerox determined it wanted to be a world-class competitor, it benchmarked every process to determine how to make that process the best in its class.

Comparisons of attributes can be made by either a direct competitive comparison of strengths and weaknesses or benchmarking that studies comparable processes in any other organization. Benchmarking is a learning experience that "steals shamelessly" from friend and foe alike. When Ford benchmarked six other well-run companies, it found the following key attributes: executives spent time outside their offices communicating with employees; people and their skills were a competitive advantage; trust replaced controls; cross-functional teams developed cutting-edge products and services; bureaucracy was out and teams were in; authority was delegated; training was readily available; and each benchmarked company said it was customer driven.

As people on a benchmarking team observe successful new practices elsewhere, they become enthusiastic champions of change. For example, when an international electronics company benchmarked its plants by function, benchmarking teams found several plants had extremely efficient manufacturing processes. The people involved in the benchmarking activity championed the rapid acceptance of the more efficient processes throughout the organization.

A *Fortune* 500 company benchmarked attributes other large organizations considered key to success. The best companies listed processes that achieved results as the keys to success, while less successful ones ignored the process and simply listed the results—as though each was unaware of the fact that process performance determines results.

Companies that compete using customer data, employing CRM (customer relationship management) techniques, are regularly benchmarking. This very accountable branch of marketing is constantly assessing the payout of a customer offer and evaluating each offer versus other inducements. The offer with the best payback is expanded or used again. These companies are continually testing offers at a small scale to evaluate their relative effectiveness. Online retailers like Overstock.com segment their customer base and benchmark offers against different groups of customers to build more refined targeting and even better results.

LOOK FOR STRATEGIC TURNS—TRANSLATION

Sun Tzu continues:
Having paid attention to the advantages of my stratagems, *the commander must create a helpful situation over and beyond the ordinary rules.* * By "situation" I mean he should act expediently in accordance with what is advantageous in the field and so meet any exigency.

All warfare is based on deception. Therefore, when able to attack, we must pretend to be unable; when employing our forces, we must seem inactive; when we are near, we must make the enemy believe we are far away; when far away, we must make him believe we are near.

Offer a bait to allure the enemy, when he covets small advantages; strike the enemy when he is in disorder. If he is well prepared with substantial strength, take double precautions against him. If he is powerful in action, evade him. If he is angry, seek to discourage him. If he appears humble, make him arrogant. If his forces have taken a good rest, wear them down. If his forces are united, divide them.

> Launch the attack where he is unprepared; take action when it is unexpected.
>
> These are the keys to victory for a strategist. However, it is impossible to formulate them in detail beforehand.
>
> Now, the commander who gets many scores *during the calculations in the temple*** before the war will have more likelihood of winning. The commander who gets few scores during the calculations in the temple before the war will have less chance of success. With many scores, one can win; with few scores, one cannot. How much less chance of victory has one who gets no scores at all! By examining the situation through these aspects, I can foresee who is likely to win or lose.

*The leader's responsibility in planning is explained in another translation:

> ... the general must create situations which will contribute
> to accomplishment of plans.
> —General Tao Hanzhang

**Other translators use different words to describe calculations:

One says "strategic factors," another calls them "conditions," and still another translates calculations as meaning "strengths and weaknesses."

LOOK FOR STRATEGIC TURNS—MANAGER'S COMMENTARY

Develop strategies that go beyond conventional rules.

When the minutemen faced the redcoats on the open battlefield of Concord in the traditional frontal confrontation of the time, the minutemen lost. Then, the minutemen made a fundamental shift in their battle tactics and fired on the redcoats from behind stone fences as they returned to Boston. This shift in tactics initiated a strategic turn in combat, as the new strategy of skirmishing contributed to the success of the American Revolution.

Externally Focused Strategic Turns: Wal-Mart's initial strategy focused on small towns. Wherever it invaded, competitive merchandising strategy was changed forever. The advent of mass merchants like Wal-Mart at one extreme of retailing, and specialty boutiques at the other, reshaped merchandising strategies across a wide variety of industries.

ESPN is an example of a cable network that heralded a new strategy in marketing. ESPN doesn't have viewers; it has fans that make it a competitive powerhouse. Originally a network with a lot of sporting events, ESPN has reshaped itself into a network for sports junkies. It supplies sporting news and events to every single continent including Antarctica.[2]

Internally Focused Strategic Turns: At the Tactical Air Command during six and one-half years of General Bill Creech's leadership, dramatic improvements in combat readiness were made with no additional people or money. To achieve this awesome record, Creech changed the internal operating strategy to focus on decentralization of authority. His commanders immersed themselves periodically in operations—for example, spending a week with a night maintenance crew. Throughout his command, he applied the principles of quality management as outlined in his best selling book *The Five Pillars of TQM* (product, process, organization, leadership, and commitment).[3]

As a result, the combat capability of the Tactical Air Command doubled and billions of dollars were saved. Out-for-maintenance aircraft were reduced 71 percent, and monthly sorties increased 80 percent (the productivity bottom line). Fighter parts delivery time was reduced dramatically, and aircraft accident safety increased 275 percent.

Sometimes missed strategic turns become evident after business results deteriorate. For years, while Detroit automakers declined,

Toyota grew. When the 2008 financial crisis hit and Detroit automakers tumbled, Toyota initially looked to be a beneficiary of U.S. automakers' continued troubles—it continued to grow and overtook GM to become the world's largest automaker. But less than a year later, the president of Toyota said his company was one step away from "capitulation to irrelevance or death."[4] His words were reflective of the wrong strategic turn of his predecessors, who had pursued rapid growth as the auto business matured.

Chapter 2

Waging War

Strategic Rules

- Marshal Adequate Resources
- Make Time Your Ally
- Everyone Must Profit from Victories
- Know Your Craft

Since the ideal strategy is whatever works best, it follows that implementation is a powerful component of the strategic rollout. The tactical implementation plan is as important as the strategic plan because it takes the vision and strategy to the point of contact.

A European strategist, Captain Johnstone, wrote in 1916:

You do not know how the enemy is disposed? Fight and find out. The decisive attack can only be confidently fixed after some fighting. The tentative attack is not a separate fight, but the beginning of the battle. Launch a formation against the whole front and you learn the shape.[1]

With the right strategy, the battle is only half won; the strategy succeeds only with professional execution of tactics. Problems arise when planning is separated from execution. This is like separating thinking from doing and diffuses responsibility.

The important thing is to get started. Too much time spent in planning can breed indecisiveness and error. It is often better to engage in

13

some form of simultaneous planning and implementation. This can be as difficult as changing a tire while the car is moving. Tactical plans must be shaped in relation to reality with the information learned from contact.

In every endeavor, the abnormal is normal and uncertainty is certain. A contingency plan should be prepared to allow for the abnormal. The exercise of preparing the contingency plan yields insights into threats and opportunities.

Close examination of companies with great reputations for long-range planning reveals they also focus on short-term gains. That is, they play for the championship one day at a time with a consistent focus on long-range direction.

MARSHAL ADEQUATE RESOURCES—TRANSLATION

Sun Tzu says:

Generally, operations of war involve one thousand swift chariots, one thousand heavy chariots and one hundred thousand mailed troops with the transportation of provisions for them over a thousand li. Thus the expenditure at home and in the field, the stipends for the entertainment of state guests and diplomatic envoys, the cost of materials such as glue and lacquer and the expense for care and maintenance of chariots and armour, will amount to one thousand pieces of gold a day.

An army of one hundred thousand can be raised only when this money is in hand. *

*The point that funds must be available before the attack is launched is emphasized in another translation:

Only when you have in hand one thousand pieces of gold for each day can the hundred thousand troops be mobilized.

—Roger Ames

Although many translators refer to the required funds as pieces of gold, the Chinese did not have gold coins in Sun Tzu's time. The money was probably ounces of silver.

MARSHAL ADEQUATE RESOURCES—MANAGER'S COMMENTARY

Invest adequate resources so the operation can be sustained.

Home Depot, Best Buy, and other giant category killers in the retailing marketplace understand how to marshal enough resources to overwhelm the market. By combining the concentration of an overwhelming assortment of merchandise with the propaganda of everyday low prices, they suck up market share like crazy.

The cry from every business failure is, "We ran out of money," but the real problem was probably one or more of the following: not enough managerial talent or operational skill, wrong products or services, or one of myriad other inadequate resources required to make the organization successful.

The failure of many airline start-ups is an obvious business parallel to Sun Tzu's expressed need to have enough resources to survive. Often, these business failures are accompanied by an announcement that the organization ran out of capital before it could generate enough business to be profitable. So it is that all business problems eventually become financial problems. In every battle, the one with the most resources has the odds in his favor. As Damon Runyon said, "The battle may not go to the strong, or the race to the swift, but that's the way to bet."

The problem of adequate resources is especially critical in start-ups because they do not have the base of loyal customers that sustains mature businesses in an economic downturn. But all companies face choices. Paul Otellini, the current CEO of Intel, says, "Every Intel CEO makes at least one big bet." In Otellini's case, it was on the Atom mobile chip—their smallest chip ever.

To achieve success, you must have superiority. However, that superiority is always relative. It is only necessary to answer the question: What is the allowable limit of resources to allocate? If you are truly determined to win, there is no upper limit. However, this does not mean you should recklessly squander resources. When resources are depleted and cannot be replenished, the result will be bankruptcy.

MAKE TIME YOUR ALLY—TRANSLATION

Sun Tzu continues:

In directing such an enormous army, a speedy victory is the main object.

If the war is long delayed, the men's weapons will be blunted and their ardor will be dampened. If the army attacks cities, their strength will be exhausted. Again, if the army engages in protracted campaigns, the resources of the state will not suffice. Now, when your weapons are blunted, your ardor dampened, your strength exhausted and your treasure spent, neighboring rulers will take advantage of your distress to act. In this case, no man, however wise, is able to avert the disastrous consequences that ensue.

Thus, while we have heard of stupid haste in war, we have not yet seen a clever operation that was prolonged. * There has never been a case in which a prolonged war has benefited a country. Therefore, only those who understand the dangers inherent in employing troops know how to conduct war in the most profitable way.

Hence, what is valued in war is a quick victory, not prolonged operations.

---

*Crude yet quick strategies have been known. But skill has yet to be observed in prolonged operations.
—R. L. Wing

Speed Wins

Throughout history, winning generals developed disciplines and systems for moving faster than their opponents. Napoleon's troops marched at 120 paces per minute while his opponents marched at 70 paces; speed alone gave Napoleon an advantage that contributed to his success.

Sun Tzu's point is not that speed can overcome stupidity. Operations must be completed rapidly because when actions take too long, the chance increases for errors and unforeseen events to contribute to failure.

MAKE TIME YOUR ALLY—MANAGER'S COMMENTARY

The key is to become rapidly effective and efficient.

Cisco and Salesforce.com are examples of fast-moving companies that won early strong positions in technology: computer networking and business-to-business CRM. Internally, cycle-time reduction and just-in-time systems have increased the effectiveness and efficiency of production.

Some businesses in traditional industries have used the Internet to dramatically change industry cycle times. Ponoko.com lets consumers order furniture and craft products over the Internet and doesn't begin production until someone orders one. Individual production is sourced, via the Internet, to a producer with the capability to manufacture the product and get it to consumers quickly.[2]

A speedy victory is indeed the main objective, and the value of time, being a little ahead of your opponent, has contributed to many victories. Achieving this advantage involves both getting started quickly and rapidly attaining a position of strength.

Building strength rapidly is, in itself, a clever advantage either because you take the opponent unaware or because the swift concentration of multiple elements creates the force of simultaneous action. So it is that the first one to the river usually crosses without difficulty.

The speed with which a position is occupied is critical. Those who own a position early may need to expend fewer resources defending it than those who come later and must try to occupy that position. The defense of an occupied position is always less costly than the expenditure required to take that position.

Because the high cost of acquiring new customers depletes financial resources more rapidly than the cost of keeping existing customers, new business ventures must move rapidly to build a loyal customer base.

Here are a few key issues in making time an ally:

- As a rule, earliest is best. Time saved is time gained.
- The later you start, the more you require.
- The more urgent the need for a decision, the longer it takes.
- Rapid decision making produces rapid execution.
- Rapid action is simultaneous action.
- Delayed decisions inevitably lose their positive quality.
- All the positive consequences of speed accrue to the early offensive.
- The less you delay:
    - the less apt you are to be surprised
    - the less ready will be your competitor
    - the greater the probability your time of attack will be earlier than expected

As a result, your opponent will be surprised and the consequences will accrue in your favor.[3]

EVERYONE MUST PROFIT FROM VICTORIES—TRANSLATION

Sun Tzu continues:

Those adept in employing troops do not require a second levy of conscripts or more than two provisionings. They carry military supplies from the homeland and make up for their provisions relying on the enemy. Thus the army will be always plentifully provided.

When a country is impoverished by military operations, it is because an army far from its homeland needs a distant transportation. Being forced to carry supplies for great distances renders the people destitute. On the other hand, the local price of commodities normally rises high in the area near the military camps. The rising prices cause financial resources to be drained away. When the resources are exhausted, the peasantry will be afflicted with urgent exactions. With this depletion of strength and exhaustion of wealth, every household in the homeland is left empty. Seven-tenths of the people's income is dissipated and six-tenths of the government's revenue is paid for broken-down chariots, worn-out horses, armour and helmets, arrows and crossbows, halberds and bucklers, spears and body shields, draught oxen and heavy wagons.

Hence, a wise general is sure of getting provisions from the enemy countries. One zhong of grains obtained from the local area is equal to twenty zhong shipped from the home country; one dan of fodder in the conquered area is equal to twenty dan from the domestic store.

Now in order to kill the enemy, our men must be roused to anger; to gain the enemy's property, our men must be rewarded with war trophies. Accordingly, in chariot battle, when more than ten chariots have been captured, those who took the enemy chariot first should be rewarded. Then, the enemy's flags and banners should be replaced with ours; the captured chariots mixed with ours and mounted by our men. The prisoners of war should be kindly treated and kept. This is called "becoming stronger in the course of defeating the enemy."

EVERYONE MUST PROFIT FROM VICTORIES— MANAGER'S COMMENTARY

Strengthen human resources and material assets with each victory.

In companies funded through private equity that have not yet declared an Initial Public Offering, employees sign up for below-market salaries in the hope of large payouts when the company goes public. Most times, of course, these hopes end up dashed. But there are well-known stories of a few of these that worked: Google's IPO is one of the best known, enriching many early employees. The hope of large rewards motivates employees and aligns their personal financial well-being with the success of the company. In these organizations, attracting the best people depends on the ability of the company to convince prospective employees of the likelihood of the big payout.[4]

While I was visiting the national headquarters of one of America's most successful companies, one of its major competitors announced it was going out of business. Within minutes, you could hear secretaries on the phone advising branch managers to immediately interview and hire the best of the now-defunct competitor's salespeople (who would also have contacts with the best prospects). As Sun Tzu says, "This is called 'becoming stronger in the course of defeating the enemy.'" What a loss of good fortune it would be to win the battle and not become stronger.

Too often, a corporate acquisition results in a "housecleaning" of very competent and experienced people. The people who are terminated in the interest of financial efficiencies are often those who really know the customers, the culture, and the subtle elements necessary for success. Because these experienced people are terminated, the acquired company becomes weaker before it becomes stronger, if it survives at all.

The acquisition strategy of many successful companies has been to keep the original owners and staff of acquired companies as active managers while providing the financial resources to power future growth. The chairman of a successful business built on friendly acquisitions said, "One of the key objectives in an acquisition is to retain the existing management. They are the people who built the business, and if we are going to buy that business, it is important to utilize their strengths."

The opportunity to profit from victories also applies to internal recognition and reward programs. Think about providing opportunities for everyone to win. Make the award cycle short and issue rewards immediately after the event. Always gather an audience when you give recognition.

KNOW YOUR CRAFT—TRANSLATION

Sun Tzu continues:
   And therefore the general who understands war is the controller of his people's fate and the guarantor of the security of the nation.

Qualities of Leadership

Thousands of years ago, one of Sun Tzu's commentators, Ho Yen-hsi, wrote, "The difficulties in the appointment of a commander are the same today as they were in ancient times"[5]—and that was said during what we consider ancient times.

Napoleon in his maxims said, "It is exceptional and difficult to find in one man all the qualities necessary for a great general. That which is most desirable, and which instantly sets a man apart, is that his intelligence or talent are balanced by his character or courage. If his courage is the greater, the general heedlessly undertakes things beyond his ability. If, on the contrary, his character or courage is less than his intelligence, he does not dare carry out his plans."

Mao Tse-tung wrote, "In actual life we cannot ask for an invincible general; there have been few such generals since ancient times. We ask for a general who is both brave and wise; who usually wins battles in the course of war—a general who combines wisdom with courage."

British Major General J. F. C. Fuller writes about a competitive quality: "Originality, not conventionality, is one of the main pillars of generalship. To do something that the enemy does not expect, is not prepared for, something which will surprise him and disarm him morally. To be always thinking ahead and to be always peeping round corners. To spy out the soul of one's adversary, and to act in a manner which will astonish and bewilder him, this is generalship."

Military writers also agree that an important quality of an ideal leader is a concern for people. In *On the Psychology of Military Incompetence,* Dixon points out that humanitarianism is a prerequisite for high morale and physical health.

KNOW YOUR CRAFT—MANAGER'S COMMENTARY

Master the expertise required to win.

When *Fortune* magazine lists the ten most admired companies, it generally recognizes the leadership of each. In general, the most admired companies have strong and stable leadership people who know their business well. Look at the most recent top five companies on this list and the length of tenure of their CEOs.

1. **Apple** Steve Jobs spent decades with Apple and has been CEO since 1997.
2. **Berkshire Hathaway** Warren Buffet has been at the helm for more than forty years.
3. **General Electric** Jeffrey Immelt has been CEO for almost a decade.

4. **Google** Eric Schmidt has been CEO since 2001, but the company has only been around since 1998.

5. **Toyota** Katsuaki Watanabi has been CEO for just four years, but he has been a company employee for forty-five years (typical of Toyota CEOs, who come from within and serve four to six years).

Many of the star executives of top companies are long-time experts in their craft; they have succeeded in their current roles as well as in other roles in their companies or industries.

When the early Romans built an aqueduct, the engineer who designed the structure stood under it when the scaffolding was removed. His expertise in his craft truly determined whether he lived or died.

Computer people should run computer companies (witness the disastrous short term of John Scully when he moved from Pepsi to Apple); beverage people should run beverage companies; and airline people should run airline companies. The credentials of an industry expert are impressive: Who would argue about coffee with Starbucks founder Harold Schultz or motorcycles with Harley-Davidson turnaround leader Vaughn Beals?

The trio in Tampa who opened the first of over 500 Outback Steakhouses had years of restaurant experience with Steak & Ale, Bennigan's, and Chili's and at the New Orleans World's Fair. This Australian concept restaurant has become one of the most popular and profitable steakhouses of the 1990s.[6]

Any venture capitalist will tell you that the background and character of the people is the most important factor in the success of a new venture.

Chapter 3

Attack by Stratagem

Strategic Rules

- Win Without Fighting
- Strength Against Weakness—Always
- Beware of "High-Level Dumb"
- Obey Fundamental Principles

At every level of any operation, strategy is indeed "war on a map"—it is the "plan on paper." Strategy deals with the allocation of resources to the battle. In *On War,* Clausewitz says that strategy sets the point *where,* the place *when,* and the *force with which* the battle is to be fought.

In his book *Strategy,* B. H. Liddell Hart explains the objective of strategy: "The true aim is not so much to seek battle as to seek a strategic situation so advantageous that if it does not of itself produce the decision, its continuation by battle is sure to achieve this."[1]

The first rule in strategy is to pay painstaking attention to the needs and wants of the customer, and your organization's ability to fulfill those needs. This analysis includes every step from design through delivery and after-sale service. Only after a thorough analysis of your ability to meet the customers' needs do you check with competitive realities to determine the viability of your strategy. Great strategy never reacts to the competitor; instead, strategy defines the opportunity in terms of the customer and then considers the situation in the competitive environment. Strategy must also consider the depth of corporate resources, effect of government regulations, environmental concerns, and currency fluctuations.

Strategy is not a competitive game. "Do more, better, faster" is not a strategy. Strategy focuses on adding real value to the customer. Strategy does not seek confrontation; instead, it seeks to achieve objectives with minimum combat.

Great strategies arise from intense discussion and deliberation that take into account internal strengths and weaknesses and external threats and opportunities. This thorough analysis provides insights that can identify important strategic opportunities.

WIN WITHOUT FIGHTING—TRANSLATION

Sun Tzu says:

Generally, in war the best thing of all is to take the enemy's state whole and intact; to ruin it is inferior to this. To capture the enemy's entire army is better than to destroy it; to take intact a battalion, a company or a five-man squad is better than to destroy them. Hence, to win one hundred victories in one hundred battles is not the acme of skill. To subdue the enemy without fighting is the supreme excellence.

Thus, the best policy in war is to attack the enemy's strategy. The second best way is to disrupt his alliances through diplomatic means. The next best method is to attack his army in the field.

The worst policy is to attack walled cities. Attacking cities is the last resort when there is no alternative.

It takes at least three months to make mantlets and shielded vehicles ready and prepare necessary arms and equipments. It takes at least another three months to pile up earthen mounds against the walls. The general unable to control his impatience will order his troops to swarm up the wall like ants with the result that one third of them are slain, while the cities remain untaken. Such is the calamity of attacking walled cities.

> Therefore, *subdue the enemy's army without fighting. They capture the enemy's cities without assaulting them and overthrow his state without protracted operations.* *
>
> Their aim must be to take all under heaven intact through strategic superiority. Thus, their troops are not worn out and their triumph will be complete. This is the art of attacking by stratagem.

*Sun Tzu's Strategy Applied to Business

Subdue the enemy's army without fighting: Find a nonconfrontational strategy.

Capture the enemy's cities without assaulting them: Use an indirect approach.

Overthrow his state without protracted operations: Win without expending excessive time or resources.

WIN WITHOUT FIGHTING—MANAGER'S COMMENTARY

The ultimate victory is to win without conflict.

Alamo Car Rental's first market entry was in the least crowded (and least alluring) niche of tour operators who purchased auto rentals at wholesale rates. Enterprise Rent-A-Car found a different point of entry into the same business. Originally a leasing company, it began an entry into rental cars when an enterprising manager at one of its offices began picking up customers for the start of their lease. No one else did that, and that became Enterprise's point of entry.

Across the television spectrum are companies who carved out a niche where there was limited competition: CNN in news, HGTV in home and garden ideas, MTV in music for the younger generation, the

History Channel in documentaries, and the list goes on. Everyone with a new product or business concept has rushed to expand rapidly and capture markets ahead of competition.

The concept of being victorious without engaging in conflict is fundamental to Sun Tzu's strategic thought. To apply this concept, it is necessary to seek victory before entering the competitive arena. Otherwise, you must fight in the hope of winning. This concept of winning before the battle applies to every situation. We so often find that the outcome has really been determined before the battle. This is expressed in the saying, "The side that wins will be the side that has already won."

Strategy is a *planning* process. It is war on paper. It is doing the right thing. It is seeking victory before the battle.

Tactics is a *contact* process. It is the action of the war. It is doing things right. It is the battle.

The best organizations develop win-win strategic initiatives. They do their planning (strategy) so well they are sure to win. When competitive forces are encountered, their implementation (tactics) is so good they win anyway.

STRENGTH AGAINST WEAKNESS—ALWAYS—TRANSLATION

Sun Tzu continues:
Consequently, the art of using troops is this:
When 10 to the enemy's one, surround him.
When five times his strength, attack him.
If double his strength, engage him.
If equally matched, be capable of dividing him.
If less in number, be capable of defending yourself.
And if in all respects unfavorable, be capable of eluding him.
Hence, a weak force will eventually fall captive to a strong one if it simply holds ground and conducts a desperate defense. *

*Other translators' versions of the last sentence help explain the consequences of fighting a larger foe:

> A small force is but booty for one more powerful.
> —Samuel B. Griffith

> Thus a small enemy that acts inflexibly
> will become captives of a large enemy.
> —Ralph D. Sawyer

> For if inferior numbers make a determined stand,
> they will be captured by the greater.
> —A. L. Sadler

> Though an obstinate fight might be made by a smaller force,
> in the end it must be captured by the larger force.
> —James Clavell

Note the phrases of warning to the smaller force: "if it simply holds ground," "acts inflexibly," makes "a determined stand," and "an obstinate fight." All suggest that guerrillas must be mobile and ready to "bug out" when outmatched.

STRENGTH AGAINST WEAKNESS—ALWAYS —MANAGER'S COMMENTARY

Battles are won by concentrating strengths.

In America, Gillette will sell the most razorblades, Frito-Lay will sell the most potato chips, and Anheuser-Busch the most beer. The reason is they have more locations selling razorblades, potato chips, or beer.

Their location strength is backed up with all the necessary strength of production and distribution.

Operations succeed because someone knows how to concentrate strengths against weaknesses. The rule of ratios of strengths is simple: If we do not have real superiority, we cannot win. The objective is not an equal match; seek an unequal advantage in your favor. As Napoleon said, "God is on the side of the heaviest artillery."

The issue is not one of raw numbers; superiority can be achieved in a variety of ways. In business competition, the superiority can be in elements of the marketing mix such as place (locations or shelf space), price, promotion, product, etc. Superiority can also be attained in the fighting spirit of the organization.

It is vital to know the strengths and weaknesses of our opponent in order to assess where the attack must be focused. Underestimate the opponent and the results can be disastrous.

The use of simple mathematical ratios to indicate when one should launch the offensive has a real application to every strategic situation. When you have overwhelming superiority, you will win. When the other side has overwhelming superiority, it will win. Between these two extremes are a variety of situations where extended combat will be required.

Much of success in any endeavor can be achieved by focusing your resources where you can achieve decisive results profitably; you cannot be strong everywhere. This requires a careful analysis of both profit opportunities and market needs. The priority ranking is important. First, you must satisfy the needs of the market. Then, and only then, can you profit from your actions. When the profit requirements are first, you have the wrong decision sequence. The decision on the needs of the market is always made before the financial decision. It's done successfully no other way.

As you think about applying strength, think seriously about reinforcing your own strength. This is often the best way to win.

BEWARE OF "HIGH-LEVEL DUMB"—TRANSLATION

Sun Tzu continues:

Now, the general is the bulwark of the state:

If the bulwark is complete at all points, the state will surely be strong.

If the bulwark is defective, the state will certainly be weak.

Now, there are three ways in which a sovereign can bring misfortune upon his army:

1. By ordering an advance while ignorant of the fact that the army cannot go forward, or by ordering a retreat while ignorant of the fact that the army cannot fall back. This is described as "hobbling the army."

2. By interfering with the army's administration without knowledge of the internal affairs of the army. This causes officers and soldiers to be perplexed.

3. By interfering with direction of fighting, while ignorant of the military principle of adaptation to circumstances. This sows doubts and misgivings in the minds of his officers and soldiers.

If the army is confused and suspicious, neighboring rulers will take advantage of this and cause trouble. This is simply bringing anarchy into the army and flinging victory away.

Orders Versus Instructions

In the Prussian armies of the late nineteenth century, a system was instituted to clearly differentiate between orders and instructions:

- **Instructions** were an expression of the commander's wishes, not to be carried out unless manifestly practicable.
- **Orders** were to be obeyed instantly and to the letter.

However, orders could be issued only by an officer *actually present with the troops concerned and fully aware of the situation.*[2]

This clear differentiation provides a methodology to ensure headquarters does not run operations by remote control.

BEWARE OF "HIGH-LEVEL DUMB"—MANAGER'S COMMENTARY

Avoid acting without full knowledge of the situation.

The financial collapse of 2008 was presaged by a naïve confidence in the financial system and the mechanisms to control risk. A few years before the almost-meltdown, Alan Greenspan, then head of the Federal Reserve, said, "*I believe that the general growth in large [financial] institutions have occurred in the context of an underlying structure of markets in which many of the larger risks are dramatically I should say, fully hedged.*" We later learned the risk inherent in big financial institutions, particularly those deemed "too big to fail." The risks that remained in the system, despite Greenspan's reassurances, came close to creating a financial collapse.

In *The Reckoning,* David Halberstam's book on the auto industry, he articulates the problem of "men whose strength was that they could hear the truth in their own voices." Halberstam says, "There were, it was believed, few honest answers at Ford during McNamara's years because there were few honest questions." When managers do not ask the right questions, the answers do not make any difference, creating "high-level dumb" situations.

Do not sow the seeds of destruction by micromanaging. There are a variety of alibis for this behavior; none are valid! No subordinate can operate at a level of competency when the boss supervises every detail. Over one hundred years ago, Marshal Saxe wrote about generals who wish to do everything on the day of battle and as a result do nothing. Saxe says, "If the general wishes to be a sergeant-major and be everywhere, he will act like the fly in the fable who thought it was he that was driving the coach."

When management is incompetent, good people simply "fire their boss" by leaving the organization. High turnover rates can be a signal of trouble.

In *On the Psychology of Military Incompetence,*[3] author Norman Dixon cites anxiety as the most common cause of leadership failure. He theorizes that what has been taken for lack of intelligence was perhaps due to the crippling effects of anxiety on perception, memory, and thought.

Dixon identifies personal faults common to incompetence:

- A fundamental conservatism and clinging to outworn tradition
- A tendency to reject or ignore information
- A tendency to underestimate the opponent
- Indecisiveness
- A failure to make use of surprise
- A predilection for frontal assaults
- A failure to make adequate reconnaissance

Too often, incompetent leaders resist new information because it might cause them to change their course of direction. The greater the impact of the new information, the more strenuously it is resisted because if changes must be made, then they were wrong before.

OBEY FUNDAMENTAL PRINCIPLES—TRANSLATION

Sun Tzu continues:
Thus, there are five points in which victory may be predicted:

1. He who knows when to fight and when not to fight will win.

2. He who understands how to handle both superior and inferior forces will win.

3. He whose ranks are united in purpose will win.

4. He who is well prepared and lies in wait for an enemy who is not well prepared will win.

5. He whose generals are able and not interfered with by the sovereign will win.

It is in these five points that the way to victory is known. Therefore, I say:

Know the enemy and know yourself, and you can fight a hundred battles with no danger of defeat.

When you are ignorant of the enemy but know yourself, your chances of winning and losing are equal.

If ignorant both of your enemy and of yourself, you are sure to be defeated in every battle.

Sun Tzu's Fundamental Principles Adapted for Business

1. **Understand when to launch the offensive.** Good information sources will help you know when to take offensive action and when to withhold it.

2. **Allocate resources.** Use different strategies when inferior and superior.

3. **Plan a united effort.** Secure a common belief at all levels in a common vision.

4. **Take advantage of opportunities.** Be prepared to act when others are unprepared.

5. **Decentralize.** Each unit leader must know her area and be empowered with authority.

OBEY FUNDAMENTAL PRINCIPLES—MANAGER'S COMMENTARY

**The chances for failure are high
when the rules that ensure victory are ignored.**

Here are a few fundamental principles of business:

Organize an Intelligence System: Know your market as well as you know yourself. Decision making must be data driven.

Maintain Objectives: Determine a clear direction and keep a steady aim. Do not wander down side tracks.

Establish a Secure Position: Strengthen your core competencies. Occupy a position that cannot easily be taken by your opponent.

Keep on the Offensive: Being on the offensive preserves freedom of action and keeps you in control.

Plan Surprise: This is the best way to gain psychological dominance and deny the initiative to your opponent. Speed is an essential component of surprise.

Think Maneuver: Consider how to put yourself at an advantage and your opponent at a disadvantage. Find lightly defended or unoccupied competitive positions.

Concentrate Resources: Mass sufficiently superior force at the decisive place and time. Be a guerrilla when you can't be a gorilla. The strongest at any given time and place will always defeat the weakest.

Practice Economy of Force: When you concentrate somewhere, you will be weak in other areas.

Keep It Simple: The simple works best. Even the simplest plans can be difficult to execute.[4]

These fundamental principles of business are guidelines that lead to success. Although principles can sometimes be violated, they must always be considered. To know the principles and violate them is to take risks. To ignore the principles is stupidity. Violate these principles only when you *know* you are violating them. The further you stray from the fundamental truths, the greater the risks.

Applying the principles is an art. It is in this art that judgment comes into play. Professionals are aware of the subtleties of business rules; amateurs too often ignore the rules. Both take risks; both win and lose. Only one has the odds in his favor. The greater the experience the professional manager has, the greater his understanding the risks of straying from the principles and the less his tendency to stray without a valid reason.

Chapter 4

Disposition of Military Strength

Strategic Rules

- Be Invincible
- Attain Strategic Superiority
- Use Information to Focus Resources

In business discussions, the issue constantly arises: Does strategy determine tactics or is it tactics that determines strategy? Strategy *always* comes before tactics, just as thinking comes before doing. However, thinking can be the easy part; it's the doing that is difficult.

It is a business fundamental that the strategy must be correct for the tactics to succeed. There's no chicken and egg problem here; the strategy must be right first, you must be *doing the right thing*. Then the tactics can support the strategy by *doing things right*. Excellent strategy at higher levels can sustain many tactical failures at lower levels. The converse is rarely true. Sustained tactical success—even continuous brilliant execution of tactics—seldom overcomes an inadequate strategic posture.

A bad strategy supported by good tactics can be a fast route to failure as, for example, driving fast and skillfully in the wrong direction will not get you to your destination. Success requires a balance of strategy and tactics. History proves that the best strategy and tactics are achieved in areas fundamental to the core strengths of the organization.

Strategy must consider tactics, and successful tactical implementation requires an appreciation of strategy. Otherwise, the tactician will not understand why he is doing what. When we do not understand the underlying concepts, we do not have the ability to improve or improvise properly.

BE INVINCIBLE—TRANSLATION

Sun Tzu says:

The skillful warriors in ancient times first made themselves invincible and then awaited the enemy's moment of vulnerability. Invincibility depends on oneself, but the enemy's vulnerability on himself. It follows that those skilled in war can make themselves invincible but cannot cause an enemy to be certainly vulnerable. Therefore, it can be said that, one may know how to achieve victory, but cannot necessarily do so.

Invincibility lies in the defense; the possibility of victory in the attack. Defend yourself when the enemy's strength is abundant, and attack the enemy when it is inadequate. *

Those who are skilled in defense hide themselves as under the most secret recesses of earth.

Those skilled in attack flash forth as from above the topmost heights of heaven.

Thus, they are capable both of protecting themselves and of gaining a complete victory.

*Other translators offer different interpretations of invincibility:

So we see that the great general can protect himself from giving the enemy an opportunity for victory, but he cannot make the enemy susceptible to defeat.
—Brian Bruya

Invincibility is a matter of defense, vulnerability is a matter of attack.
Defense is for times of insufficiency, attack is for times of surplus.
—Thomas Cleary

Security against defeat implies defensive tactics; ability to defeat the
enemy means taking the offensive. Standing on the defensive indicates
insufficient strength: attacking a superabundance of strength.
—Lionel Giles

Defend yourself when you cannot defeat the enemy, and attack the enemy
when you can. One defends when his strength is inadequate; he attacks
when it is abundant.
—General Tao Hanzhang

BE INVINCIBLE—MANAGER'S COMMENTARY

Build strengths that can take advantage of opportunities.

The invincible awards in American business go to companies like
Microsoft, with its take-no-prisoners attitude; McDonald's, which is
everywhere; and Starbucks, who owns the high ground in gourmet coffee. They may have off years, but their industry leadership positions
have yet to be seriously challenged.

A common characteristic of these premier organizations is a strong
founding leader who set the direction and kept the organization on
course. Strong companies are founded by strong individuals—when
they leave, the stamp of their culture becomes the core of the organization's future.

At Ogilvy & Mather, founder David Mather established the practice
of sending each new branch head a nested set of wooden dolls—each
doll opens to reveal a smaller replica of the doll. Inside the smallest is

a message: "If each of us hires people who are smaller than we are, we shall become a company of dwarfs; but if each of us hires people who are bigger than we are, Ogilvy & Mather will become a company of giants."[1]

Personal leadership is where "art" takes over to control the application of "science." This does not mean that principles are ignored, but rather that the successful leader understands how to properly apply the principles.

No leader does it alone. As Kets de Vries points out in *Life and Death in the Executive Fast Lane:* "The derailment of a CEO is seldom caused by a lack of information about the latest techniques in marketing, finance, or production; rather, it comes about because of a lack of interpersonal skills—a failure to get the best out of people who possess necessary information."

Coca-Cola has a chief learning officer whose job is to figure out how to institutionalize the sharing of experiences between branch offices, countries, and people, and to turn Coke into a "learning organization." Google offers "20 percent time" to their engineers, company time that they can spend working on corporate projects they are personally passionate about. "The ability to learn faster than your competitors may soon be the only sustainable competitive advantage," says Arnie De Geus, head of planning at Royal Dutch Shell.[2]

ATTAIN STRATEGIC SUPERIORITY—TRANSLATION

Sun Tzu continues:

To foresee a victory no better than ordinary people's foresight is not the acme of excellence. Neither is it the acme of excellence if you win a victory through fierce fighting and the whole empire says, "Well done!" Hence, by analogy, to lift an autumn hair [hare] does not signify great strength; to see the sun and moon does not signify good sight; to hear the thunderclap does not signify acute hearing.

In ancient times, those called skilled in war conquered an enemy easily conquered. Consequently, a master of war wins victories without showing his brilliant military success, and without gaining the reputation for wisdom or the merit for valor. He wins his victories without making mistakes. Making no mistakes is what establishes the certainty of victory, for it means that he conquers an enemy already defeated.

Accordingly, a wise commander always ensures that his forces are put in an invincible position, and at the same time will be sure to miss no opportunity to defeat the enemy. *It follows that a triumphant army will not fight with the enemy until the victory is assured, while an army destined to defeat will always fight with the opponent first, in the hope that it may win by sheer good luck.* The commander adept in war enhances the moral influence and adheres to the laws and regulations. Thus it is in his power to control success.

*Other translators emphasize the importance of strategic planning:

Thus, a victorious army wins its victories before seeking battle; an army destined to defeat fights in the hope of winning.
—Samuel B. Griffith

So we see, the victorious person creates the conditions for certain victory and then does battle with the enemy. The defeated person always engages the enemy first, then hopes he is lucky enough to win.
—Brian Bruya

ATTAIN STRATEGIC SUPERIORITY—MANAGER'S COMMENTARY

A successful strategy achieves victory before the battle.

There is a long history of the successful entry of products where competition was minimal or nonexistent: Xerox into copiers, IBM into data analysis, Apple into home computers, and Crest with fluoride toothpaste. With this kind of superiority, the initial competitive battle was quite limited in scope.

Milwaukee-based Kohl's has cut a wide swath in soft goods retailing with a leadership dedicated to a carefully crafted strategy. A stock analyst says, "Kohl's combines the cost structure of a discounter and the brands of a department store. It straddles those worlds and takes share from both." The design and merchandising is not too upscale and not too low rent. The shopper finds a clean, bright store where everything is easy to find. The service is good and the perceived value is high.[3]

The introduction of Tide detergent by Procter & Gamble involved a classic strategy of gaining brand name superiority. When automatic washers first came to market, manufacturers were anxious to educate new purchasers to use detergent instead of soap, which would leave a scum in places that could not be cleaned. So P&G provided leading producers with free boxes of Tide to be packed in every automatic washer at the factory. The free trial experience convinced many to become repeat customers. And Tide became the leading detergent brand without engaging in a major conflict.

Although all conflict cannot be avoided, a well-planned strategy will nullify most opposition. Fighting and winning requires less strategic skill than winning without fighting.

Opportunities for attaining strategic superiority can be found in:

- The product or service that is so clearly unique and carefully targeted that it is has no competition

- The idea that is so completely researched and validated that no other seems viable
- The fundamental truth that is presented with such moral strength that any other approach appears immoral

The issue is always how one's strategy can win the customer and nullify the opposition. The offensive should never be aimed at the opponent's strengths. Strategies that focus on the customer's needs and consider the opponent's weaknesses have the best odds for winning.

USE INFORMATION TO FOCUS RESOURCES—TRANSLATION

Sun Tzu continues:
Now, the elements of the art of war are first, the measurement of space; second, the estimation of quantities; third, the calculation of figures; fourth, comparisons of strength and fifth, chances of victory. *

Measurements of space are derived from the ground. Quantities derive from measurement, figures from quantities, comparisons from figures, and victory from comparisons.

Therefore, a victorious army is as one yi balanced against a grain, and a defeated army is as a grain balanced against one yi.

An army superior in strength takes action like the bursting of pent-up waters into a chasm of a thousand fathoms deep. This is what the disposition of military strength means in the actions of war.

*Other translators clarify:

The art of war may be summarized into five steps:
First, survey of terrain features;
Second, decision of the plan of campaign;
Third, calculation of man-power;

Fourth, weighing of chances;
Fifth, deliberation on victory.

—Tai Mien-leng

According to The Art of War, there are five processes of preparation:

1. to control,
2. to produce,
3. to compare,
4. to determine,
5. to win.

—Tang Zi-chang

USE INFORMATION TO FOCUS RESOURCES— MANAGER'S COMMENTARY

Use data to plan overwhelming advantages.

When Robert Nardelli was president of General Electric's power systems unit, he asked his top 100 customers about their most critical needs and how GE could provide solutions. The answers prompted the company to drastically reduce its response time for providing parts. It also opened the opportunity to advise utilities on the nuances of expanding into foreign markets that were new to them but not to GE.[4]

Many online advertisers use customer data to present more relevant ads to prospects. Online search-engine marketing may be the most targeted marketing ever developed. In general, the more relevant the recommendations the higher the sales from those communications so the performance of the data to make decisions that drive sales is highly tracked and managed.

Organizations that have added only customer input to their historic financial measurements have not completed their system. Although the customer input adds another dimension, the financial measures only serve to keep score on what has happened. More is needed.

The solution is to focus on defining and aligning performance in several key areas: financial, customer, employee, process, innovation, and learning. With achievement of the corporate strategy as the main objective, supportive objectives are established for each key performance area at every level of the organization. Then, a measurement system to track performance is cascaded so that everyone is aligned to achieve the desired results. This cascading measurement system, often called a balanced or synchronized scorecard, encourages the kind of performance that achieves results in areas critical to success.

This balanced system of measurements is a dynamic, continuous activity where all processes are aligned with strategy. To put it simply, linking your vision to performance improves productivity and profit potential.

Chapter 5

Use of Energy

Strategic Rules

- Build a Sound Organization Structure
- Apply Extraordinary Force
- Coordinate Momentum and Timing

There are two basic command systems for the use and control of energy in the attack:

Centralized control—Reinforcing weakness: Imagine a field of battle where the commander monitors the front line to see where he is winning and losing. When he sees that one of his units is losing, he sends in reserves to strengthen the weakness. This system of reinforcing weakness requires a high degree of control.

Decentralized control—Reinforcing strength: In this situation, as offensive forces move forward, they attempt to bypass strengths instead of engaging in battle. If the offensive forces meet opposition, they go around again and again until they find a place they can penetrate. The front-line commander does not ask for permission to advance; he merely reports while the senior commander and his staff monitor and support the advance. This decentralized control reinforces strength.[1]

The decision to use a system of centralized or decentralized control depends on the mental set of the senior officers and the corporate culture. Whether the culture tolerates one system or the other has a great deal to do with success.

Someone must be in charge. Where everyone decides everything, no one decides anything. Rule by committee can become rule by mediocrity. Chaos is the inevitable result when decisions are made by everyone. Clearly expressing his views on command, Napoleon wrote to the National Assembly stating that one bad general is preferable to two good ones.

Be careful! The ability of modern communications to reach everywhere can make it too easy to concentrate all power in a single person, who through overwork is often over his head.

No one command system is best. Command systems radically different from each other have led to equally good results.

BUILD A SOUND ORGANIZATION STRUCTURE—TRANSLATION

Sun Tzu says:

Generally, management of a large force is the same in principle as the management of a few men: it is a matter of organization. And to direct a large army to fight is the same as to direct a small one: it is a matter of command signs and signals. *

*In general, commanding a large number is like commanding a few. It is a question of dividing up the numbers. Fighting with a large number is like fighting with a few. It is a question of designation and configuration.
—Ralph D. Sawyer

Organizational Warnings

In 210 B.C., Petronius Arbiter wrote: "We trained hard, but it seemed that every time we were beginning to form up in teams we would be reorganized. I was to learn later in life that we tend to meet any new situation by reorganizing, and a wonderful method it can be for creating the illusion of progress while producing confusion, inefficiency, and demoralization."

Over 100 years ago, a French officer, Ardant du Picq, warned:

Note the army organizations and tactical formations on paper are always determined from a mechanical point of view, neglecting the essential coefficient, that of morale. They are almost always wrong . . . . Mental acquaintanceship is not enough to make a good organization. A good general esprit is needed.

In his book *Generalship: Its Diseases and Their Cure*, J. F. C. Fuller wrote: "The horde army paralyzed generalship, not so much because it changed tactics, but because it prevented tactics changing."

Discussing the resulting staff structure, he said, "The general alone is responsible, therefore the general alone should and must decide and must elaborate his own decisions and not merely have them thrust on him by his staff like a disc upon a gramophone."

BUILD A SOUND ORGANIZATION STRUCTURE— MANAGER'S COMMENTARY

The organization exists so that tasks can be managed, people supported, and results achieved.

At Harley-Davidson, the organization chart has been described as three overlapping circles: a Create Demand Circle responsible for marketing and sales; a Produce Products Circle for engineering and production; and a Support Circle for all other functions. In the middle, where the circles intersect, is a Leadership and Strategy Council that oversees general management functions like planning, budgeting, and human relations. The overlapping of the circles emphasizes the interdependence between areas and encourages participation and collaboration.[2]

No single organization structure works everywhere.

Change managment consultant Gerald Sentell says, "Structure is to an organization as channels are to river systems. They direct and control flows of human interaction and activity . . . . When the structure can contain and direct the flows of behavior, the system functions. When the flows jump out of the structured channel, the results can create great change."[3]

When organizations are structured to maximize strengths within departments, the result can disrupt the overall optimization of the organization. When departments are organized to serve themselves, the sum total of these departmental kingdoms is not maximized to serve the customer, and business is lost to competitors who know how to focus strengths on the customer.

Systems and processes should not be designed to accommodate the strengths and weaknesses of individuals. Instead, the requirements of the system determine where people are placed in the structure.

Structure follows strategy, always. First determine the strategy to achieve your vision and then develop the organization structure. Finally, put the best people in place.

APPLY EXTRAORDINARY FORCE—TRANSLATION

Sun Tzu continues:

That the whole army can sustain the enemy's all-out attack without suffering defeat is due to operations of extraordinary and normal forces. Troops thrown against the enemy as a grindstone against eggs is an example of the strong beating the weak.

Generally, in battle, use the normal force to engage and use the extraordinary to win. Now, to a commander adept at the use of extraordinary forces, his resources are as infinite as heaven and earth, as inexhaustible as the flow of the running rivers. They end and begin again like the motions of the sun and moon. They die away and then are reborn like the changing of the four seasons.

There are not more than five musical notes, but the various combinations of the five notes bring about more melodies than can ever be heard.

There are not more than five basic pigments, yet in blending them together it is possible to produce more colors than can ever be seen.

There are not more than five cardinal tastes, but the mixture of the five yields more flavors than can ever be tasted.

In battle, there are not more than two kinds of postures—operation of the extraordinary force and operation of the normal force, but their combinations give rise to an endless series of maneuvers. For these two forces are mutually reproductive. It is like moving in circle, never coming to an end. Who can exhaust the possibilities of their combinations?

*Translators offer a variety of meanings for what this version calls the normal and the extraordinary:

- One translates the Chinese ideograms as meaning "direct and indirect"—that is, use the direct to engage, the indirect to win.
- Another calls the normal force "regular operations" and the extraordinary force "surprise."
- Still another says, *In fighting you engage the foe with the main body and defeat him with the reserves.*

APPLY EXTRAORDINARY FORCE—MANAGER'S COMMENTARY

Use the normal to engage, the extraordinary to win.

Frito-Lay knows how to apply extraordinary force at the point of sale with drivers who restock customers' shelves with uncommon frequency.

With the extraordinary force of over 2 million agents knocking on doors, Avon is the world's number one direct seller of cosmetics. Cyberspace is turning storefront retailing into the normal force and Internet retailing into the extraordinary.

Virgin and its founder, Richard Branson, are masters of the extraordinary. From the publicity generated by luxurious airport lounges and comfortable airplane seating to headline-grabbing stunts like hot-air ballooning, Branson knows how to use the extraordinary to build a brand image and extend it to music, airlines, mobile cellular service, vodka, financial services, and tourist space travel.

This powerful idea of moving from the normal to the extraordinary achieves results at every level and in every situation. The classic human relations case study occurred years ago at the Bell Lab Hawthorne plant when researchers determined that giving extraordinary attention to a small group of workers increased production. This study concluded that production went up regardless of whether working conditions were enhanced or made worse. The key was the extraordinary attention. Today, results are being achieved by people-oriented activities that apply the extraordinary. It may be as simple as applying teamwork to problem solving, finding new ways to get commitment, or initiating training programs.

The idea of using the extraordinary is an extremely simple concept that clearly identifies what must be done to win. Too often, our plans are based on using only the normal force and the result is that only "normal" results are achieved. Every annual plan that simply adds "some effort" to what was done last year is only another plan. It takes the force of extraordinary effort to achieve extraordinary results.

The idea of using extraordinary force does not mean more of the same effort. Extraordinary action results from out-of-the-box thinking. Major General J. F. C. Fuller writes, "If we wish to think clearly, we must cease imitating. If we wish to cease imitating, we must make use of our imagination. Audacity and not caution must be our watch word."

COORDINATE MOMENTUM AND TIMING—TRANSLATION

Sun Tzu says:

When torrential water tosses boulders, it is because of its momentum; when the strike of a hawk breaks the body of its prey, it is because of timing.* Thus, in battle, a good commander creates a posture releasing an irresistible and overwhelming momentum, and his attack is precisely timed in a quick tempo. The energy is similar to a fully drawn crossbow; the timing, the release of the trigger. Amid turmoil and tumult of battle, there may be seeming disorder and yet no real disorder in one's own troops. In the midst of confusion and chaos, your troops appear to be milling about in circles, yet it is proof against defeat.

Apparent disorder is born of order; apparent cowardice, of courage; apparent weakness, of strength. Order or disorder depends on organization and direction; courage or cowardice on postures; strength or weakness on dispositions.

Thus, one who is adept at keeping the enemy on the move maintains deceitful appearances, according to which the enemy will act. He lures with something that the enemy is certain to take. By so doing he keeps the enemy on the move and then waits for the right moment to make a sudden ambush with picked troops.

Therefore, a skilled commander sets great store by using the situation to the best advantage, and does not make excessive demands on his subordinates. Hence he is able to select the right men and exploits the situation. He who takes advantage of the situation uses his men in fighting as rolling logs or rocks. It is the nature of logs and rocks to stay stationary on the flat ground, and to roll forward on a slope. If four-cornered, they stop; if round-shaped, they roll. Thus, the energy of troops skillfully commanded is just like the momentum of round rocks quickly tumbling down from a mountain thousands of feet in height. This is what "use of energy" means.

*Other translations of the first sentence:

That the velocity of cascading water can send boulders bobbing about is due to its strategic advantage. That a bird of prey when it strikes can smash its victim to pieces is due to timing.
—Roger Ames

The onset of troops is like the rush of a torrent which will even roll stones along its course. The quality of decision is like the well-timed swoop of a falcon which enables it to strike and destroy its victim.
—Lionel Giles

COORDINATE MOMENTUM AND TIMING— MANAGER'S COMMENTARY

Momentum provides force; timing applies strength at the right moment.

Subway opened over 10,000 stores in the eighties and nineties in the United States. They maintained their momentum and a high rate of franchisee growth by shifting to an international focus in the nineties and the first decade of this century, and now have more than 25,000 stores worldwide. In many countries, they operate more outlets than McDonald's.

Nothing succeeds like success, and success generates its own momentum. Even in the difficult recession economy of 2009, Toyota maintained the momentum of its pioneering hybrid Prius with an aggressively marked introduction that created waiting lists while other car companies saw double-digit declines of all their models.

Just as volume sales create momentum and enthusiasm, obsolete inventory stifles innovation and growth. When the cash register rings, it seems like you are doing everything right; when it doesn't ring, the mistakes are very visible.

Successful strategic thrusts are achieved by rapidly accumulating power (momentum) and releasing that power when it will have the most desirable effect (timing). A typical business application would be the introduction of a very competitive new product or the implementation of a major change in warranty or pricing at a major trade show, when it would be most disruptive of a competitor's plans.

Momentum and timing are most often combined in advertising campaigns where massive expenditures are timed with seasonal demand. Or as an associate often said when we discussed timing of a major event, "Let's go hunting when the birds are flying."

The simultaneous use of multiple principles or techniques, a concept the military refers to as force multipliers, can apply a lot of pressure. It is not that victory is achieved with the application of a single principle, but rather the use of multiple principles achieves a reinforcing momentum. The cumulative effort of doing a lot of right things right multiplies into awesome power! This happens when retailers move into a new market with multiple locations featuring extensive selections and engage in enough advertising to make them a super power in the media.

Chapter 6

Weakness and Strength

Strategic Rules

- Take the Initiative
- Plan Surprise
- Gain Relative Superiority
- Seek Knowledge
- Be Flexible

Achieving real superiority is fundamental to the concept of strength against weakness. Your strategy and tactics must be designed with the idea that your competitor will not have anywhere near an equal chance to win. Strategically, the concentration of strength against weakness is a mental process. Tactically, this concentration is a physical act.

Here are key methodologies for concentrating strength against weakness:

Flank: Concentrate strength against weakness by launching an end run around strong points to a lightly defended or unoccupied position. In your search for weakness, consider these two key elements:

1. Look for weakness at a junction. It can be between geographic locations or product lines. Also explore going around the extreme low end or high end of a product category.

2. Since every strength has a corresponding weakness, look for the weakness of the opposition's strength.

Segment: This is concentrating strength in a specific area. The small can never equal the big everywhere, but anyone can be strong somewhere. As markets have been segmented and resegmented, marketers discover new ways to concentrate against weakness and then concentrate again into a smaller niche or particular market.

Overwhelm: Any initiative can be achieved if enough strength is concentrated to support it. Conversely, any initiative can be defeated if enough strength is focused against the weakness of that initiative.

Reinforce: The best odds for success are achieved by spending time, money, and energy reinforcing what is working. Then you are leveraging off what you do well.

TAKE THE INITIATIVE—TRANSLATION

Sun Tzu says:

Generally, he who occupies the field of battle first and awaits his enemy is at ease; he who arrives later and joins battle in haste is weary. And, therefore, one skilled in war brings the enemy to the field of battle and is not brought there by him. *

One able to make the enemy come of his own accord does so by offering him some advantage. And one able to stop him from coming does so by inflicting damage on him.

Therefore, on the day the decision is made to launch war, you should close the passes, destroy the official tallies, and stop the passage of all emissaries. Examine the plan closely in the temple council and make final arrangements.

If the enemy leaves a door open, you must rush in. Seize the place the enemy values without making an appointment for battle with him.

> Be flexible and decide your line of action according to the situation on the enemy side.
>
> At first, then, exhibit the coyness of a maiden until the enemy gives you an opening; afterwards be swift as a running hare, and it will be too late for the enemy to oppose you.

*The one who first decides on the battleground and there awaits the enemy has the easier task, and the one who comes after and has to hurry will tire himself. The good fighter makes others move, but is not made to move by them.
—A. L. Sadler

Seize and Maintain the Initiative

Mao Tse-tung wrote, "No military leader is endowed by heaven with an ability to seize the initiative. It is the intelligent leader who does so after a careful study and estimate of the situation and arrangement of the military and political factors involved."

In *The Foundations of Strategy,* Captain Johnstone warned, "The initiative, once handed over to the enemy, is hard to regain: Ward off blows for a week and your hands are full of defensive details, you begin to be apprehensive of the unseen work of the enemy, and you abandon your plan on small provocation."

TAKE THE INITIATIVE—MANAGER'S COMMENTARY

By its very nature, the offensive offers an advantage for gaining superiority.

Minnesota Mining & Manufacturing (3M) strives to generate one-third of its sales revenues from new products that did not exist four years ago. In a single year, 3M received over 500 U.S. patents for new products. It accelerates sales with a Pacing Plus initiative that rapidly develops and markets the most promising new products aimed at high-growth industries.

In a relatively short time, Wal-Mart has become the world's largest retailer. Its low-price, low-cost model allowed Wal-Mart to first take the initiative in the United States and later in overseas markets. The company first entered the mass-market channel, then added food and built the first national chain of Supercenters. Recent initiatives include a strong dot.com presence and Hispanic-format stores.

The most effective and decisive way to reach the objective is to seize, retain, and exploit the initiative. Being on the offensive puts you in control and forces the opponent to react.

Taking the initiative is first a strategic mental process followed by real tactical action. By acting first, we preserve freedom of action. If our opponent moves first, our only choice may be to react.

The attack has the advantage of initiative. It often forces action on our opponent and relegates him to second place. Initiating the offensive adds positive morale to our side.

The keys to the successful initiative are skill, preparation, and information. The norm is not enough time, not enough resources, not enough information. Consequently, the initiative often requires that "great mental leap in the dark."

Only rarely will exact details be known. While the attempt to get more information is made as a matter of course, waiting for news in a difficult situation is a bad error. While data is needed to launch the offensive, normally the sooner that something is done the better the odds in your favor and the better the results.

Beware! The offensive does not offer a solution to all problems. Your desire for action must be matched by wisdom.

PLAN SURPRISE—TRANSLATION

Sun Tzu continues:

Thus, when the enemy is at ease, he is able to tire him; when well fed, to starve him; when at rest, to make him move. All these can be done because you appear at points that the enemy must hasten to defend.

That you may march a thousand li without tiring yourself is because you travel where there is no enemy.

That you are certain to take what you attack is because you attack a place the enemy does not or cannot protect.

That you are certain of success in holding what you defend is because you defend a place the enemy must hasten to attack.

Therefore, against those skillful in attack, the enemy does not know where to defend, and against the experts in defense, the enemy does not know where to attack. *

How subtle and insubstantial that the expert leaves no trace. How divinely mysterious that he is inaudible. Thus, he is master of his enemy's fate.

His offensive will be irresistible if he plunges into the enemy's weak points; he cannot be overtaken when he withdraws if he moves swiftly. Hence, if we wish to fight, the enemy will be compelled to an engagement even though he is safe behind high ramparts and deep ditches. This is because we attack a position he must relieve.

If we do not wish to fight, we can prevent him from engaging us even though the lines of our encampment be merely traced out on the ground. This is because we divert him from going where he wishes.

*Another translator expands on how to confuse opponents:

Thus, an ingenious attacker makes the defender at a loss how to defend; an ingenious defender makes the attacker at a loss how to attack.
—Zhang Huimin

PLAN SURPRISE—MANAGER'S COMMENTARY

Blend subtlety and secrecy to keep the opponent confused so he knows neither where to attack or defend.

Southwest Airlines often waits until the last moment to announce plans to extend its routes to new markets so the competition has little time to prepare.

Secrecy about your own movements can be more threatening to competitors than overt action. Some manufacturers have a corporate policy of no public announcement preceding a new product introduction. Since the unknown often appears more threatening than the known, this secrecy becomes a powerful and threatening ally. Concerning corporate raider Rupert Murdoch, a Wall Street analyst said, "Part of Murdoch's strategy is to play his cards close to his vest. The magic is secrecy."

Secrecy protects your plans, while surprise confuses your opponent. In business, it is not essential that your opponent be taken unaware, but only that he becomes aware too late to react effectively. In that case, your opponent will probably announce that he "misread the market."

Even though your current position may be weak, you can do things to divert the enemy from your position. This kind of bluff is achieved by starting rumors that work to your advantage.

The objective of surprise is to obtain a psychological dominance that denies the initiative to your opponent. Sheridan said the reason for Grant's victories in the Civil War was that, "while his opponents were kept fully employed wondering what he was going to do, Grant was thinking most of what he was going to do himself." When surprise is achieved, the balance of power will often be decisively shifted. As a result, success earned from surprise greatly exceeds the effort expended.

Speed is an essential component of surprise. The longer you take, the more likely your opponent will be aware of your actions. Focus on rapid, hard-hitting thrusts aimed at your opponent's weakness.

GAIN RELATIVE SUPERIORITY—TRANSLATION

Sun Tzu continues:

Accordingly, by exposing the enemy's dispositions and remaining invisible ourselves, we can keep our forces concentrated, while the enemy's must be divided. We can form a single united body at one place, while the enemy must scatter his forces at 10 places. Thus, it is 10 to one when we attack him at one place, which means we are numerically superior. And if we are able to use many to strike few at the selected place, those we deal with will be in dire straits.

The spot where we intend to fight must not be made known. In this way, the enemy must take precautions at many places against the attack. The more places he must guard, the fewer his troops we shall have to face at any given point.

For if he prepares to the front his rear will be weak; and if to the rear, his front will be fragile. If he strengthens his left, his right will be vulnerable; and if his right gets strengthened, there will be few troops on his left. If he sends reinforcements everywhere, he will be weak everywhere.

Numerical weakness comes from having to prepare against possible attacks; numerical strength from compelling the enemy to make these preparations against us.

Relative Superiority Wins

The concept of relative superiority can be distilled from Sun Tzu's statement: "*. . . we can keep our forces concentrated, while the enemy's must be divided.*" Another translation is worded: "*. . . if I concentrate while he divides, I can use my entire strength to attack a fraction of his.*"

In the first millennium during the Song dynasty, China had the biggest and strongest army in the world. However, the leaders did not trust their army and ignored Sun Tzu's advice on concentration by splitting their forces between capital and border armies. As a result, they lost to the Mongol invaders, who could concentrate their strength against fractions of the Chinese.

In *On War,* Clausewitz says, "Where absolute superiority is not attainable, you must produce a relative one at the decisive point by making skillful use of what you have."

GAIN RELATIVE SUPERIORITY—MANAGER'S COMMENTARY

Deploy resources to concentrate strengths against weaknesses.

In the eighties and nineties, the "Killer Bs," Barnes & Noble and Borders, killed off most locally owned bookstores. Their large stores, extensive selections, discounted prices, and ambience provided a shopping experience that the local bookseller could not generally match. Bookstores that continue to thrive found a niche where they could achieve relative superiority. In a megastore built long before the chains came to Portland, Oregon, Powell's main bookstore stocks 200,000 titles of new books plus 300,000 used books. In a unique merchandising set, new and used books are stacked side by side so readers find an awesome selection in every category. Says Michael Powell, "One way to survive is simply to be bigger and offer a more diverse stock than they do."[1]

In the last decade, the dominance of the Killer Bs has been deeply challenged by Amazon. Using the Internet, Amazon built a relative advantage by being an early Internet retailer, achieving a strong position as overall Internet usage grew. Then they built technology for a new personal service using knowledge of every item their customers purchased, giving them an opportunity to build competitive advantage using that data to the benefit of their customers. Today, Amazon's personal-recommendation software is heavily emulated by other Internet retailers and gave Amazon leverage as they expand beyond books.

Their Kindle ebook reader provides yet another opportunity to take relative superiority and again redefine book retailing.

An inferior force can think strategically about winning if it can tactically achieve relative superiority at each point of contact. This is the way small companies become big companies and competitors in every endeavor become champions. This is the way guerrillas win—they find out where the enemy is weak and overwhelm him at that point.

When you attempt to concentrate everywhere, you have no concentration. The more thoroughly you specialize, the more sure you are to win. Winning strategies amass resources on the main effort and allocate minimal resources to secondary efforts.

Relative superiority is the best strategy for most companies. Although relative superiority is most often thought of as weight of numbers, there is a variety of ways to achieve relative superiority:

- Implementing continuous action—for example, consistent, small ads
- Segmenting by finding a niche or specific market
- Concentrating on your own strengths
- Forming an alliance—for example, joining a franchise
- Achieving superior product or service quality

When you cannot have absolute superiority, you must concentrate your strengths against your opponent's weaknesses to achieve relative superiority. It's a business fundamental that you must focus your resources where you can achieve decisive results profitably.

SEEK KNOWLEDGE—TRANSLATION

Sun Tzu continues:

Therefore, if one knows the place and time of the coming battle, his troops can march a thousand li and fight on the field. But if one knows neither the spot nor the time, then one cannot manage to have the left wing help the right wing or the right wing help the left; the forces in the front will be unable to support the rear, and the rear will be unable to reinforce the front. How much more so if the furthest portions of the troop deployments extend tens of li in breadth, and even the nearest troops are separated by several li!

Although I estimate the troops of Yue as many, of what benefit is this superiority in terms of victory?

Thus, I say that victory can be achieved. For even if the enemy is numerically stronger, we can prevent him from fighting.

Therefore, analyze the enemy's battle plan, so as to have a clear understanding of its strong and weak points. *Agitate the enemy so as to ascertain his pattern of movement. Lure him in the open so as to find out his vulnerable spots in disposition. Probe him and learn where his strength is abundant and where deficient.* *

Now, the ultimate in disposing one's troops is to conceal them without ascertainable shape. In this way, the most penetrating spies cannot pry nor can the wise lay plans against you.

*Here is another translator's version of getting more knowledge about your opponent's plans:

Scheme so as to discover his plans and the likelihood of success. Rouse him, and learn the principle of his activity and inactivity. Force him to reveal himself, so as to find out his vulnerable spots. Carefully compare the opposing army with our own, so that you may know where strength is superabundant and where it is deficient.

—Tang Zi-chang

SEEK KNOWLEDGE—MANAGER'S COMMENTARY

Knowledge helps stack the odds in your favor.

When Ford introduced the Taurus, engineers tore apart competitors' cars to find features to adapt. In an extensive research campaign, Ford went to end customers and dealers' sales and service personnel to find out what customers wanted. Eventually, a want list of over 1,400 items was generated. About 50 percent of these "wants" were incorporated in the Taurus, which became one of the hottest selling new cars of its time.

Knowledge of the current situation makes it possible for victory to be created. As Patton said, "Intelligence is like eggs: the fresher, the better."

Here are active ways to produce the kinds of knowledge about your opponent that help determine the correct strategy for winning:

- **Watch what he is doing.** As Yogi Berra said, "You can see a lot by observing."
- **Watch what he is not doing.** This is key to obtaining relative superiority.
- **Probe.** This reveals the opponent's strengths and weaknesses.
- **Benchmark.** This gets people involved in finding out how to develop the best processes.

Centuries ago, Ovid wrote, "It is right to learn, even from the enemy."

Basic to success in business is being close to the customer. That's why executives visit the marketplace; they realize they must not only understand how the customer thinks, they must be able to think like a customer. It is essential to know what your customer wants. The idea of gathering and analyzing information before the battle hasn't been tried and found wanting; it's been found difficult and not tried.

In the timeless classic *The Exceptional Executive,* Levinson says, "A professional is a person who must understand and apply scientific knowledge. Unless he does so, he will be buffeted by forces beyond his control. Given knowledge, the professional can choose courses of action. He is in charge of himself and his work." Absolutely nothing beats using data to make decisions.

BE FLEXIBLE—TRANSLATION

Sun Tzu continues:

Even though we show people the victory gained by using flexible tactics in conformity to the changing situations, they do not comprehend this. * People all know the tactics by which we achieved victory, but they do not know how the tactics were applied in the situation to defeat the enemy. Hence no one victory is gained in the same manner as another. The tactics change in an infinite variety of ways to suit changes in the circumstances.

Now, the laws of military operations are like water. The tendency of water is to flow from heights to lowlands. The law of successful operations is to avoid the enemy's strength and strike his weakness. Water changes its course in accordance with the contours of the land. The soldier works out his victory in accordance with the situation of the enemy.

Hence, there are neither fixed postures nor constant tactics in warfare. He who can modify his tactics in accordance with the enemy situation and thereby succeeds in winning may be said to be divine. Of the five elements, none is ever predominant; of the four seasons, none lasts forever; of the days, some are longer and others shorter, and of the moon, it sometimes waxes and sometimes wanes.

*Other translators give their interpretations of the need for flexibility:

Perfectness of military movement lies in variation; it is beyond the prying of subtle spies and the machinations of wise brains.
—Tai Mien-leng

Victory is won by flexibly coping with circumstances. If you lay this fact before the people, they will find it hard to comprehend.
—Zhang Huimin

BE FLEXIBLE—MANAGER'S COMMENTARY

While strategies remain constant, tactics must be adapted to each new situation.

Recessions provide great opportunities for the nimble to cheaply, opportunistically improve their market position. In 2009, when Sun Microsystems spurned IBM's takeover bid, Oracle quickly swooped in and purchased Sun for just a dime a share more than IBM's final offer. In the same year pharmacy benefits Manager Express Scripts significantly improved their market position with the acquisition of a significant rival that, according to one expert, gave Express Scripts 'considerable negotiating clout' versus their rivals.

The opposite side of the coin of flexibility is rigidity. When we are rigid, we are predictable. In competitive battles, predictability can be a weakness. Being predictable can signal your intended actions to your opponent, and the odds of failure increase.

Winning isn't easy; it requires simultaneous planning and action. While preliminary planning is important, too much planning can be deadly. All plans are merely the basis for change. Revise plans in relation to what is happening and make adjustments as you go.

The blitzkrieg (lightning war) used so successfully by the German army in World War II is an adaptation of Sun Tzu's comments about the flow of water around obstacles. The blitz is launched along a wide front with the objective of rapid penetration. When resistance is met, the forces go around until they can get through. This strategy was applied by General Norman Schwarzkopf, commander of the allied forces in Iraq during the First Gulf War.

The blitz in any business operation works the same way. It is a concentrated effort in a short period of time with the objective of going around resistance and focusing resources where results can be attained. The blitz requires a high degree of decentralization. Forget remote approvals; the successful blitz is an empowered front-line offensive with results that can far exceed any ordinary effort. You can find the "lightning war" concept applied throughout organizations in everything from a productivity-oriented kaizen blitz to a volume-oriented sales blitz.[2]

Chapter 7

Maneuvering

Strategic Rules

- Maneuver to Gain the Advantage
- Achieve the Critical Mass
- Deceive Your Competitor
- Develop Effective Internal Communications
- Gain the Mental Advantage

At the strategic level, maneuvering is a way of thinking about how you are going to act in a manner that puts your opponent at a disadvantage. At the tactical level, maneuvering most frequently involves concentrating or dispersing as you seek the most advantageous route. Without thinking about how to maneuver, the idea of fighting when outnumbered is ludicrous.

The way to avoid what is strong is to attack what is weak. Look for lightly defended positions. Engage in a frontal attack only when you have overwhelming superiority. However, sheer numbers and firepower alone are often not enough to dislodge a competitor in an entrenched position.

Look for situations where real superiority can be attained. In business, as in any battle, the best approach is most often the one that achieves superiority at the decisive point. The marketing maneuver is often an indirect approach to where your customers are and your competitors aren't.

One of the best maneuvers can be to relocate the battle. When an advertising executive arrived at a presentation, he found his client thinking of hiring a new agency. He switched from his prepared presentation to a discussion of what the client needed to do to succeed. Afterward, he commented, "I didn't even talk about the competitive account; I merely changed the battleground."

In all disagreements, including corporate political situations, thinking about maneuvering turns the mind to options. It takes the focus away from confrontation and refocuses on selecting a route that increases the odds of winning. The best win is a maneuver to a win-win.

MANEUVER TO GAIN THE ADVANTAGE—TRANSLATION

Sun Tzu says:

Normally, in war, the general receives his commands from the sovereign. During the process from assembling the troops and mobilizing the people to deploying the army ready for battle, nothing is more difficult than the art of maneuvering for seizing favorable positions beforehand. *What is difficult about it is to make the devious route the most direct and to turn disadvantage to advantage.* * Thus, forcing the enemy to deviate and slow down his march by luring him with a bait, you may set out after he does and arrive at the battlefield before him. One able to do this shows the knowledge of artifice of deviation.

Thus, both advantage and danger are inherent in maneuvering for an advantageous position.

---

*The difficulty in battles is in turning the circuitous into the straight and turning reverses into advantages.
—A. L. Sadler

Here are military maneuvers adapted for business:

Frontal attack: Head-on attack with overwhelming superiority.

Attack in echelon: Initiate the attack with the strongest products or services; then follow up with weaker ones.

Flanking attack: Attack lightly defended or unoccupied positions.

Blitz: A concentrated effort that keeps on moving as strong points are bypassed.

Encirclement: Launch a variety of competitive products and/or deny key resources to your opponent.

Fabian: Refuse to compete in certain areas, attack in others.

Defense: Maintain position against competitive thrusts.

Relocate the battle: Find a new competitive arena.

Guerrilla: Find a niche and take what you can get when you can get it.

Retreat: Get out of business.

General Pogo's Strategy: He said, "We have met the enemy and they is us." Attack yourself first.[1]

MANEUVER TO GAIN THE ADVANTAGE— MANAGER'S COMMENTARY

The longest way around can be the shortest route to success.

Major victories have been won by doing the impossible through the impassable. By figuring out how to do the impossible of getting a package from one office to another overnight, Federal Express founder Fred Smith maneuvered to a unique position in the market. When competition began encroaching on FedEx's "overnight turf," it redefined overnight to mean "before 10:30 a.m." At the same time, FedEx set up a tracking program so it could rapidly answer questions concerning the en-route location of every package. By innovating this system of early delivery and tracking, FedEx established difficult obstacles for competitors who wanted to achieve parity in service. FedEx has continued its maneuvers to provide services that give it an advantage. Years ago, Smith laid out an overarching strategy for these maneuvers and others since when he said, "The information about the package is as valuable as the package itself."

Since the easiest routes are often the most heavily defended, the longest way around can indeed be the shortest way home. The course of action that appears most advantageous usually contains the seeds of disadvantage. For example, if you take too long to organize you will probably arrive too late; however, if you are not organized your efforts will be too fragmented to win.

The key to success is turning a circuitous route into a straight route for you alone. Move rapidly; the longer you are en route, the more difficult it may be to get your resources to the market before your competitor.

Extended warranties have been a successful maneuver to a position of product or service superiority for many organizations. Although this works only until your competitor establishes parity, it can be a preemptive maneuver to win customers.

ACHIEVE THE CRITICAL MASS—TRANSLATION

Sun Tzu continues:
One who sets the entire army in motion with impedimenta to pursue an advantageous position will be too slow to attain it. If he abandons the camp and all the impedimenta to contend for advantage, the baggage and stores will be lost.

It follows that when the army rolls up the armor and sets out speedily, stopping neither day nor night and marching at double speed for 100 li to wrest an advantage, the commander of three divisions will be captured. The vigorous troops will arrive first and the feeble will

> straggle along behind, so that if this method is used only one-tenth of the army will arrive. In a forced march of 50 li the commander of the first and van division will fall, and using this method but half of the army will arrive. In a forced march of 30 li, but two-thirds will arrive. Hence, the army will be lost without baggage train; and it cannot survive without provisions, nor can it last long without sources of supplies.
>
> One who is not acquainted with the designs of his neighbors should not enter into alliances with them. Those who do not know the conditions of mountains and forests, hazardous defiles, marshes and swamps, cannot conduct the march of an army. Those who do not use local guides are unable to obtain the advantages of the ground.

Strategic initiatives can be either sequential or cumulative:

A *sequential initiative* requires planned consecutive steps to achieve success. A new product launch requiring orderly introduction to the sales force, trade channels, and end customers would most often be a sequential strategy. So would a plan to initiate a new program over time in successive units.

A *cumulative initiative* is the result of a series of random actions piling on top of one another until at some undetermined point the critical mass is reached. The brand manager who uses sponsorship and events to build brand awareness is often using a cumulative strategy, as is the plant manager who initiates a quality campaign in units throughout the plant.[2]

ACHIEVE THE CRITICAL MASS—MANAGER'S COMMENTARY

Apply overwhelming force at the decisive place and time.

Companies that compete sometimes form alliances to achieve sufficient mass in a particular area. In the United States, Google, Yahoo, and Microsoft are competitors; but as players in international information, they sometimes run into common criticism for their actions in countries that restrict free speech such as China. To give themselves protection from these criticisms in their profitable Western markets, these three companies jointly announced a set of principles on how to do business in nations that restrict free expression and speech. Said Google about these companies' agreement, "Common actions by these diverse groups is more likely to bring about change in government policy than the efforts of any one company or group acting alone." True, but this joint action will also give these businesses the critical mass to achieve greater PR protection in the core countries they draw their profits from.

For years, one of the major buying decisions of gasoline station owners was which brand of gasoline pump to buy. Then as the convenience store component of the gas station emerged, these storeowners found they needed merchandise sales recorded through a software system. The gas pump (hardware) buying decision became secondary to the more important software buying decision that provided a full range of inventory and sales information. Many companies in the computer hardware business have been beaten by companies who understood the importance of being in the software business. Strategic initiatives must focus on the critical factors that give you a competitive advantage. When you have a unique enough advantage, you should be able to get a significant portion of the market.

The critical mass is simply the concentration of energy required to achieve success. What counts is not only the strength of resources but the speed with which it is delivered. That energy concentration can be in any facet of the organization; for example, purchasing, production, marketing, distribution, etc. Nike is one of the world's most recognized brand names, and it sells more than $15 billion of shoes and other sports apparel and equipment each year, yet owns no factories. They have concentrated on design and marketing and achieved the decisive advantage in those areas.

In business as in nuclear fission, a concentration of energy must be attained to achieve the critical mass. The manager must focus her energy on performance of the tasks most critical to success.

DECEIVE YOUR COMPETITOR—TRANSLATION

Sun Tzu continues:

Now, war is based on deception. Move when it is advantageous and change tactics by dispersal and concentration of your troops.* When campaigning, be swift as the wind; in leisurely march, be majestic as the forest; in raiding and plundering, be fierce as fire; in standing, be firm as the mountains. When hiding, be as unfathomable as things behind the clouds; when moving, fall like a thunderclap. When you plunder the countryside, divide your forces. When you conquer territory, defend strategic points.

Weigh the situation before you move. He who knows the artifice of deviation will be victorious. Such is the art of maneuvering.

*Other translators clarify the meaning of deception:

In warfare, practice dissimulation, and you will succeed. Move only if there is a real advantage to be gained. Whether to concentrate or divide your troops, must be decided by circumstances.
—Lionel Giles

When waging war, you must employ cunning tactics and multiple transformations in order to succeed. You must judge whether or not something is advantageous before you act. You must decide whether to concentrate your troops or divide them according to circumstances.
—Brian Bruya

Forces achieve missions with unexpectation, take advantage to fit advantages, and create diversity through scattering and regrouping.
—J. H. Huang

DECEIVE YOUR COMPETITOR—MANAGER'S COMMENTARY

Deception is always targeted at the competitor—never the customer.

In baseball, deception is part of the surprise throw to catch the runner off base; in football, it's the hidden ball play; in basketball, it's the faked pass. Why should we consider deception unsportsmanlike in business competition?

Contemporary managers may wonder about Sun Tzu's emphasis on the importance of deception; any deceptive action might seem to be immoral. In business, the subtle difference is that deception is practiced to confuse the competitor—never the customer.

A South American company and a competitor agreed to maintain high prices on a new product both were introducing. After a few months, the competitor cut prices in violation of the agreement, causing a loss of business. When questioned, the competitor replied that it reduced prices to increase sales. The victimized company was not aware of the admonition from an ancient strategist who said, "Do not do what your enemy wants, if for no other reason than he wants it."

Much of the success of the invasion of Europe in World War II was the result of deception. This misinformation succeeded so well that when the actual invasion took place, the German officers thought the invaded beaches were the deception. You have often seen deception used as a tactic in negotiations. One side attempts to gain a psychological advantage by appearing to be naive and uninformed when, in fact, it is smart and knowledgeable. Alternatively, one side attempts to gain knowledge that the other doesn't have. Frequently, when getting a company ready for sale, companies raise prices to temporarily grow profitability and sell the business for a higher price. While this can obviously lose customers and damage the business for the long term, it can work in the short run. Savvy investors are aware of this tactic and carefully examine the books of the company they are considering buying, looking at historical as well as recent performance.

Another deceptive approach in negotiation is to appear to be dejected and crestfallen about your opportunity for prevailing. An opponent who thinks she is winning is likely to be overconfident and vulnerable.

Secrecy can also be a means of achieving deception. This forces your opponent to second-guess your next move. The bigger you are, the more psychologically threatening the unknown becomes to your opponent.

The only thing better than having your opponent not know what you are doing is to have him think you are planning to do something entirely different than what you really intend to do. This is deception. Go for it.

DEVELOP EFFECTIVE INTERNAL COMMUNICATIONS—TRANSLATION

Sun Tzu continues:

The book of Army Management says: "As the voice cannot be heard in battle, gongs and drums are used. As troops cannot see each other clearly in battle, flags and banners are used." Hence, in night fighting, usually use drums and gongs; in day fighting, banners and flags. Now, these instruments are used to unify the action of the troops. When the troops can be thus united, the brave cannot advance alone, nor can the cowardly retreat. This is the art of directing large masses of troops.

Simple Communications Work Best

In Sun Tzu's time, the only available communications were quite simple. Today, we have a wide range of communication methods available and use them all. Invariably, people at the bottom complain about lack of communication and people at the top complain about receiving more information than they can process.

With computers, the solution to more communication capacity is to break the problem into segments and look at each segment. With people, the solution is a similar decentralization: You break down the problem and achieve decisions by the people at each level instead of sending it all to the top, where you overload the head person's brain. With decentralization, you lessen the need for communication at every level.

Regardless of the level, simplicity clears the mind. Keep in mind the rule of three: never make more than three points about an issue. The problem is that long lists are confusing and, as a result, nothing is remembered. As an example, here are three facts concerning a nineteenth century Prussian command system:

1. An army cannot be effectively controlled by direct orders from headquarters.
2. The man on the spot is the best judge of the situation.
3. Intelligent cooperation is of infinitely more value than mechanical obedience.[3]

DEVELOP EFFECTIVE INTERNAL COMMUNICATIONS— MANAGER'S COMMENTARY

Implement ways to get messages received and understood.

Sears tracked the links in the chain of cause and effect running from employee attitude to customer behavior to profit. It modeled how an improvement in employee attitude changed behavior. The better behavior created an improved customer impression that resulted in a measurable increase in revenue.

Awareness of this employee-customer-profit linkage made Sears management determined to give every employee the information needed to develop an enlightened opinion about how to do her job better. Town meetings were held to spread the word and get employees initiating improvements. A corporate university was established. All of the training was focused on changing employee perceptions and attitudes so that attention and behavior would be focused on customers. As operating managers changed their behavior toward employees, front-line employees changed their behavior toward customers.[3]

Note the sequence: The change in behavior at the management level caused the change in behavior at the front line. Behavior is a form of communication; management must walk the talk.

In every industry, we receive and process so much information so fast that it's easy to hear only what we want to hear. It's becoming increasingly difficult to break through the clutter and get our message communicated to our own people.

Effective internal communication happens only as the result of a well-designed plan. This plan is organized around the understanding that all messages are not delivered in the same manner. Good news may need to be delivered only once to be heard. Instructions and changes that disrupt existing paradigms must be communicated in several different ways and often repeated before people will accept the new information. In these instances, a single method of communication is not enough; every message needs to be reinforced by using different methodologies such as one-on-one meetings, department meetings, and interactive forums.

GAIN THE MENTAL ADVANTAGE—TRANSLATION

Sun Tzu continues:

A whole army may be robbed of its spirit, and its commander deprived of his presence of mind. Now, at the beginning of a campaign, the spirit of soldiers is keen; after a certain period of time, it declines; and in the later stage, it may be dwindled to nought. *A clever commander, therefore, avoids the enemy when his spirit is keen and attacks him when it is lost.* * This is the art of attaching importance to moods. In good order, he awaits a disorderly enemy; in serenity, a clamorous one. This is the art of retaining self-possession. Close to the field of battle, he awaits an enemy coming from afar; at rest, he awaits an exhausted enemy; with well-fed troops, he awaits hungry ones. This is the art of husbanding one's strength.

He refrains from intercepting an enemy whose banners are in perfect order, and desists from attacking an army whose formations are in an impressive array. This is the art of assessing circumstances.

Now, the art of employing troops is that when the enemy occupies high ground, do not confront him uphill, and when his back is resting on hills, do not make a frontal attack. When he pretends to flee, do not pursue. Do not attack soldiers whose temper is keen. Do not swallow a bait offered by the enemy. Do not thwart an enemy who is returning homewards. When you surround an army, leave an outlet free. Do not press a desperate enemy too hard. Such is the method of using troops.

*Other translators give their interpretations of the use of morale:

A large army may be robbed of its morale and a general may be robbed of his resolution . . . a good strategist makes a point of shunning the keen morale of the enemy and does not strike him until his morale has run out.

—Zhang Huimin

So you should take away the energy of their armies, and take away the heart of their generals . . . avoid the keen energy and strike the slumping and receding.

—Thomas Cleary

GAIN THE MENTAL ADVANTAGE—MANAGER'S COMMENTARY

Understand the psychological factors affecting human resources.

Opportunities for victory are found in the mental capacity of the leader to integrate strategy (planning) and tactics (execution). The ultimate responsibility for victory or defeat lies with the leader, not because he must do everything but because he must have the mental capacity and provide the means to translate sound strategy into successful tactics.

Externally, the mental advantage is achieved through surprise. You must generate a mismatch by getting inside your adversary's observation-orientation-decision-action time cycle. By the time your adversary observes what he thinks you are doing, becomes oriented to it, decides what to do, and takes action, "it" will be too late.

Internally, several key issues are basic to good management psychology:

Attitude: A positive outlook and a cool head are the foundation of a good attitude.

Morale: Napoleon said, "The moral is to the physical as three is to one." The word "moral" refers to a worthwhile cause, a belief that what we are fighting for is just and right. It is the "moral cause" that produces high morale.

The moral issues required in business are both the moral courage to make the right decisions and act on them and the leadership style that helps make everyone feel good about herself. The business equivalent of military courage is confidence. However, confidence must be based on knowledge and experience.

Physical: Keep yourself physically fit and nurture a healthy business environment.

Adapt to circumstances: No plan can see beyond the first engagement. Although it is important to follow the plan, it is equally important to know when and how to modify the plan.

Rewards: Internal motivators include profit sharing, gain sharing, glory sharing, and fame sharing. The simple pat on the back can accomplish much.

We often hear that golf and tennis are mental games. So it is in business. The mental advantage begins with the warm confidence of a positive attitude.

Chapter 8

Variation of Tactics

Strategic Rules

- Consider Tactical Options
- Prepare Adequate Defenses
- Avoid the Faults of Leadership

S trategy determines direction. The actual execution of the plan to achieve objectives is called tactics and it begins with contact. Internally, that contact may be with the development or production process of a product or service. Externally, that contact is usually with a customer. The contact makes personal relationships an important issue in tactics and explains why tactics must vary. At the point of contact, unpredictable personal equations become part of the scenario.

While strategic principles are unchanging for all time, tactics (implementation of the strategy) vary with the times and circumstances and must be tuned to current situations.

The purpose of tactical maneuvering is to relocate the battle to a place where superiority can be obtained. In a study of 300 military campaigns, in only six was a decisive result achieved by a direct frontal approach to the main army of the enemy. Why would the results of a frontal attack be any different in other kinds of campaigns? Although the idea is appealing, the highly touted "head-on attack" has been consistently unsuccessful; the most successful tactics are usually based on some form of maneuver.

Strategies at any level are the tactics of the next lower level in the chain of command. The best tactical school is experience, and the people with prior experience in their industry have the soundest tactical foundation.

As you shape tactical options, focus on the customer. The key to success is what the customer wants, not what you can do. What ConAgra could do tactically in frozen foods was low-cost mass production. What the customer wanted was healthy foods with great taste. To develop the Healthy Choice brand to meet the customers' taste standards, ConAgra sent food technologists to the Culinary Institute. The result: a successful brand that dominates the market.

CONSIDER TACTICAL OPTIONS—TRANSLATION

Sun Tzu says:

Generally, in war, the general receives his commands from the sovereign, assembles troops, and mobilizes the people. When on grounds hard of access, do not encamp. On grounds intersected with highways, join hands with your allies. Do not linger on critical ground. In encircled ground, resort to stratagem. In desperate ground, fight a last-ditch battle.

There are some roads which must not be followed, some troops which must not be attacked, some cities which must not be assaulted, some ground which must not be contested, and some commands of the sovereign which must not be obeyed.

Hence, the general who thoroughly understands the advantages that accompany variation of tactics knows how to employ troops.

The general who does not is unable to use the terrain to his advantage even though he is well acquainted with it. In employing the troops for attack, the general who does not understand the variation of tactics will be unable to use them effectively, even if he is familiar with the Five Advantages.

> A wise general in his deliberations must consider both favorable
> and unfavorable factors. *By taking into account the favorable factors,*
> *he makes his plan feasible; by taking into account the unfavorable, he*
> *may avoid possible disasters.* *

*Other translators explain favorable factors as opportunity or advantage:

In the midst of difficulties we should ever be ready to grasp every opportunity so that our object may be obtained. In a favorable situation, we should
be alert in detecting our weakness so that we may avoid misfortune.
—Tai Mien-leng

If our expectation of advantage be tempered, we may succeed in accom-
plishing the essential part of our schemes. If, on the other hand, in the
midst of difficulties we are always ready to seize an advantage, we may
extricate ourselves from misfortune.
—Lionel Giles

CONSIDER TACTICAL OPTIONS—MANAGER'S COMMENTARY

Victory depends on our strength, which we control, and the opportunities
provided by our opponent, which we cannot control.

At Microsoft, senior managers meet nightly in a triage meeting during
the final months of the software development process. Triage is a ruth-
less assessment that determines priorities for immediate action. In the
Microsoft meeting, managers representing all perspectives are engaged
in a power interchange. People voice their point of view and the group

negotiates a decision. Tradeoffs are made clear by the key question: "Is this the hill we want to die on?" Decisions are immediately communicated so everyone can get on with his work.[1]

Philip Knight, cofounder of Nike, wrote a graduate thesis at Stanford University. The title was: "Can Japanese Sport Shoes Do to German Sport Shoes What Japanese Cameras Did to German Cameras?" A year later he was in the shoe business—the rest is history. He knew where he wanted to go and had a sense of how he could adopt different tactics in the sports shoe business. Because victory is dependent upon both our actions and those of our opponent, maximum effort does not ensure a competitive victory. This situation can be readily seen in every sporting event where maximum effort on the playing field is exerted by every participant. There are winners and losers in every game.

Tactical flexibility is the hallmark of many organizations with a reputation for customer service. That is, within guidelines, associates are empowered to take whatever action is necessary to serve the customer.

In the complexity of the business environment, an organization may be on the offensive with one product or service and on the defensive with another. The same strategies and tactics cannot be used for all circumstances. The question is how much time the manager should spend shoring up weaknesses as opposed to maximizing strengths. The options differ depending upon whether we are attacking or defending. The low-cost competitor and the high-end producer often have different core strengths requiring different tactics. The differences become obvious when you scan the advertising messages in a newspaper or magazine. Regardless of the circumstances, the spirit of the offense must always prevail. At Fort Donelson, when General Grant found his army half-routed, he galloped down the line shouting, "Fill your cartridge boxes quick and get into line; the enemy is escaping and must not be permitted to do so."

PREPARE ADEQUATE DEFENSES—TRANSLATION

Sun Tzu continues:

What can subdue the hostile neighboring rulers is to hit what hurts them most; what can keep them constantly occupied is to make trouble for them; and what can make them rush about is to offer them ostensible allurements.

It is a doctrine of war that we must not rely on the likelihood of the enemy not coming, but on our own readiness to meet him; not on the chance of his not attacking, but on the fact that we have made our position invincible. *

---

*Other translators comment on preparing a defense:

Fundamentals in the use of forces are: do not rely on their not approaching, but rely on our readiness against them; do not rely on their not attacking, but rely on our readiness which cannot be attacked.
—J. H. Huang

Do not depend on the enemy not coming; depend rather on being ready for him. Do not depend on the enemy not attacking; depend rather on having a position that cannot be attacked.
—Roger Ames

Strengthening the Defense

Strengthening the defense does not mean maintaining the status quo. General John J. (Black Jack) Pershing noted that the arrival of the airplane provided an excellent and efficient means of getting oats to horses![2] Legendary IBM CEO Thomas Watson is credited with observing, "I think there is a world market for maybe five computers."

Too often, what happens in the implementation of new military and business tools (i.e., quality management) is that the new simply overlays old doctrine and structure. World competition is a powerful new force moving quickly to challenge keepers of the old paradigm. But human nature being what it is, there will always be a struggle to maintain the status quo.

PREPARE ADEQUATE DEFENSES—MANAGER'S COMMENTARY

The best defense is a good offense.

"We will encircle Caterpillar and become the dominant producer in the industry," Komatsu declared as a key tenet of their strategic intent when they began their global expansion. Many observers predicted that Caterpillar would join the long list of American corporations that have fallen to the Japanese.

After surviving Komatsu's attack, Donald Fites, chairman and CEO of Caterpillar, said, "The biggest reason for Caterpillar's success has been our system of distribution and product support and the close customer relationships it fosters." The backbone of that system is a long history of quality relationships Caterpillar has with its world network of independent dealers. So when Komatsu's attack began, the strongest unit of defense, the dealer structure, was in place. Of course, this alone was not enough to overcome Komatsu's cost advantage; Caterpillar also had to make the organization flatter, meaner, and leaner. However, Komatsu could not overcome the marketing strength provided by Caterpillar's network of dealers with strong customer contacts. Understanding the strength of personal relationships has long been a weakness of the Japanese. The strong defense of high-quality dealer relationships and support has brought Caterpillar to the point where its share of the world market for construction and mining equipment is the highest in its history.[3]

Smaller companies or brands have achieved a good defense by owning very strong positions in a niche or particle segment of a product line or business. When they own a position in the customer's mind, they can hold off the big competitors. Witness Maker's Mark in bourbon, Danner in boots, and regional grocers or pizza parlors in your home town.

Even on the defensive, the rule is to seek every opportunity to seize the initiative and achieve results by offensive action. When you are constantly in a defensive posture, you can seldom win. Facebook found themselves in this position when they changed their Terms of Service agreement. These changes to content ownership were likely designed to give Facebook an opportunity to form a more profitable business model, but users quickly became irate, viewing it as a major privacy issue. They banded together in groups to protest this change, and major media quickly began covering the issue. Facebook took back the offensive when they rescinded those changes and concurrently announced that users would have a chance to vote on future modifications to these agreements. Facebook sets both what gets voted and the rules of these votes—they still have control—but they moved off the defensive and recreated the impression of a user-focused group.

Too often, the strategy that strengthens the defense is characterized by finding some way to redesign your existing product instead of getting out in front of the trend or technology. The mistake is to try to serve the old market in a new way instead of going where the market is growing. The defensive is not achieved by building better buggy whips.

AVOID THE FAULTS OF LEADERSHIP—TRANSLATION

Sun Tzu continues:

There are five dangerous faults* that may affect a general:

if reckless, he can be killed;

if cowardly, captured;

if quick-tempered, he can be provoked to rage and make a fool of himself;

if he has too delicate a sense of honor, he is liable to fall into a trap because of an insult;

*if he is of a compassionate nature, he may get bothered and upset.**

These are the five serious faults of a general, ruinous to the conduct of war. The ruin of the army and the death of the general are inevitable results of these five dangerous faults. They must be deeply pondered.

*Other translators' versions of the faults that may affect a general:

1. Recklessness, which leads to destruction;
2. Cowardice, which leads to capture;
3. A hasty temper, which can be provoked by insults;
4. A delicacy of honor, which is sensitive to shame;
5. Over-solicitude for his men, which exposes him to worry and trouble.

—Lionel Giles

1. Those who are ready to die can be killed;
2. Those who are intent on living can be captured;
3. Those who are quick to anger can be shamed;
4. Those who are puritanical can be disgraced;
5. Those who love people can be troubled.

—Thomas Cleary

AVOID THE FAULTS OF LEADERSHIP—
MANAGER'S COMMENTARY

**Flaws in the personal character of the commander
will cause opportunities to be lost.**

"Chainsaw" Al Dunlap got his reputation by staging massive cut-backs in personnel at Scott Paper. When the same approach didn't work at Sunbeam, he tried sales and accounting gimmicks to bolster results. Soon he was asked to exit. Jim McCann, president of 1-800-FLOWERS, tells about the lesson he learned from General Electric CEO Jack Welch. McCann had to fire a senior person that everyone knew wasn't right for the job. The guy was a friend, and the prospect of action was brutal. He met Welch at a dinner party and told him about the situation. Welch's response was, "When was the last time anyone said, 'I wish I had waited six months longer to fire that guy?'"[4]

Peers and subordinates will discover the ineffective manager long before her seniors do. The dysfunctional interactions resulting from the discovery will reduce this person's effectiveness—and the effectiveness of the organization.

Here are business parallels to Sun Tzu's character flaws:

Reckless (meaning no forethought): The reckless manager does not understand how to use data. She shoots from the hip. When a win is achieved, it is simply because she did something rather than because the right thing was done.

Cowardly (self-protective or afraid): The person who is afraid to take risks takes the greatest risk of all. This manager is like McClellan in the Civil War, who was so fearful of losing he could not win.

Quick tempered (too easily angered): Reference has been made to the importance of a cool head. Managers who have a reputation for shooting the messenger don't often get bad information and don't know what is really going on.

Delicate honor (exaggerated sensitivity): The business parallel here is being too easily embarrassed, taking things personally, or letting ego get in the way.

Too compassionate (too concerned): Those who have this fault are so concerned about the reactions of people that short-term decisions are made to keep harmony. The result is these managers end up with a long-term disaster. In their compassion people are often left "twisting slowly in the wind," when the kindest thing that could be done is to make the hard decision.

Chapter 9

On the March

Strategic Rules

- Occupy Strong Natural Positions
- Always Seek the High Ground
- Make an Estimate of the Situation
- Discipline Can Build Allegiance

Strategically, a secure position establishes a base for the offensive. Tactically, this secure position helps you use your natural strengths. Positions where you can occupy a key strong point are important in every endeavor. There are only a few leaders in each industry; everyone else marches in their shadow.

In order for a position to be secure, we must "own" it. We own a position because of a perceived strength—the perception is the reality. People accept only what is consistent with what they already know as they add to their perceptions about the position of a product or service.

All positions are in the mind, and the entry into the mind is through emotions, not logic. Logic sounds most convincing to the presenter; it is in the emotions of the receiver that positions are changed. In thinking about attacking competitive positions, the first rule is: It's very, very difficult to move into a position occupied by someone else.

To build a strong position, you must first determine what position you want and who you want your customers to be. Then figure out how you are going to meet the needs of those potential customers better than anyone else.

In business, the most secure positions are owned by those who achieve a base of loyal customers. Premier positions are earned by organizations that have systems for really listening to their customers. They then focus resources on meeting or exceeding needs in a manner that delights customers. The idea is to make customers so happy that not only do they not buy anything else, they don't even *think* of buying anything else.

However, the more secure your position seems to be, the greater the danger can be. When you feel most secure, you are most vulnerable to surprise.

OCCUPY STRONG NATURAL POSITIONS—TRANSLATION

Sun Tzu says:

Generally, when an army takes up a position and sizes up the enemy situation, it should pay attention to the following:

When crossing the mountains, be sure to stay in the neighborhood of valleys; when encamping, select high ground facing the sunny side; when high ground is occupied by the enemy, do not ascend to attack. So much for taking up a position in mountains.

After crossing a river, you should get far away from it. When an advancing invader crosses a river, do not meet him in midstream. It is advantageous to allow half his force to get across and then strike. If you wish to fight a battle, you should not go to meet the invader near a river which he has to cross. When encamping in the riverine area, take a position on high ground facing the sun. Do not take a position at the lower reaches of the enemy. This relates to positions near a river.

In crossing salt marshes, your sole concern should be to get over them quickly, without any delay. If you encounter the enemy in a salt marsh, you should take position close to grass and water with trees to your rear. This has to do with taking up a position in salt marshes.

On level ground, take up an accessible position and deploy your main flanks on high grounds with front lower than the back. This is how to take up a position on level ground. These are principles for encamping in the four situations named. By employing them, the Yellow Emperor conquered his four neighboring sovereigns.

In *The Science of War,* Colonel Henderson wrote:

"... by no means sufficient importance is attached to the selection of positions ... and to the immense advantages that are to be derived from the proper utilization of natural features."

OCCUPY STRONG NATURAL POSITIONS— MANAGER'S COMMENTARY

Find the strength of natural positions that cannot easily be occupied by your opponents.

Experienced travelers know that Jet Blue has one of the newest fleets, and because of that has televisions in every seatback of every plane—a nice convenience at no extra charge and an immediate win with customers. Challenging that position is taking competitors years because of the costs and normal replacement time of changing out existing older fleets.

Tesco dominates retailing in England the way no one company does in the United States. It got there with an everyday pricing position similar to what Wal-Mart used in the United States. It stays there by maintaining that position and using loyalty card data better than anyone else to layer on unique services that build further price and value perceptions.

Many companies are gaining strength by going back to their roots. At these core positions, they have the most inherent natural strength. In the recession that started in 2008, many companies found their natural strength to be just right for the quickly changing buying behaviors of financially shocked consumers. After losing money for a decade, Revlon found itself in the right natural position as consumers abandoned expensive department store cosmetics. When these customers arrived at the cosmetics departments of drug stores, supermarkets, and mass merchants, they found a recognizable brand in Revlon and dramatically lower prices than in department stores.

The perception of what we are is based on what we have been. Over time, the perception of what we are matches what we really are. We, ourselves, or our product or service, can't be something else. Everyone who has tried to win by copying has failed, often caused by not understanding the subtleties. To change your position in the customer's mind over time, you must change who you really are.

Efforts focused on reinforcing your natural position make it easier to communicate your position. When you say that you are what you really are, the believable message gets through to your audience.

Going up the positioning ladder to achieve a stronger share of mind requires a well-conceived and executed plan. Coming down is what happens when you are not going up. Ask any former sports star like good old "what's his name."

ALWAYS SEEK THE HIGH GROUND—TRANSLATION

Sun Tzu continues:
Generally, in battle and maneuvering, *all armies prefer high ground to low,* * and sunny places to shady. If an army encamps close to water and grass with adequate supplies, it will be free from countless diseases and this will spell victory. When you come to hills, dikes, or embankments, occupy the sunny side, with your main flank at the back. All these methods are advantageous to the army and can exploit the possibilities the ground offers.

> When heavy rain falls in the upper reaches of a river and foaming water descends, do not ford and wait until it subsides. When encountering "Precipitous Torrents," "Heavenly Wells," "Heavenly Prison," "Heavenly Net," "Heavenly Trap," and "Heavenly Cracks," you must march speedily away from them. Do not approach them. While we keep a distance from them we should draw the enemy toward them. We face them and cause the enemy to put his back to them.
>
> If in the neighborhood of your camp there are dangerous defiles or ponds and low-lying ground overgrown with aquatic grass and reeds, or forested mountains with dense tangled undergrowth, they must be thoroughly searched, for these are possible places where ambushes are laid and spies are hidden.

*Ordinarily, the force prefers heights and hates the lowlands.
—R. L. Wing

The High Ground

The most desirable position in war has always been the high ground controlling the surrounding terrain. Frederick the Great referred to selection of positions as the talent of great men—the ability immediately to conceive all the advantages of the terrain. He said, "The first rule that I give is always to occupy the heights."

ALWAYS SEEK THE HIGH GROUND—MANAGER'S COMMENTARY

The high ground is the strongest position.

The high ground in business today is owned by names with brand strength like Microsoft in software, Coca-Cola in soft drinks, Nike in athletic shoes, and McDonald's in fast foods.

Attaining the high ground is one battle and keeping it is another. In the battle for dominance of browsers in the World Wide Web, Netscape got to the high ground in market share by giving away free product. Then Microsoft entered the market with free software while Netscape started to charge for its browser, and down went Netscape's market share.

Jelly Belly, with 75 percent of the gourmet jelly bean market, increased its total sales even more by selling through major grocery chains. The concern is that this expanded distribution may affect the brand name cachet.

Each of these brands faces the problem that market share is either increasing or decreasing. There's no such thing as staying exactly where you are; you either get bigger or you get smaller.

In the military, positioning is occupying a key strong point in the terrain. In business, positioning is occupying a key strong point in the mind. You own a position in the mind either because you are the leader or because of significant differentiation. The unique taste of Dr. Pepper provides a significant differentiation.

The worst position of all may be not having a position, the problem experienced by people in the struggling brand name you've never heard of. In the final analysis, it is the perceptions of the market that actually position the brand.

In every industry, the action of moving up in market share erodes the competitor's base. This dysfunction forces displaced competitors to compete for lesser positions that offer even smaller profits. As market positions change, the one who captures higher ground gets the larger revenue base and all the accompanying advantages. Similarly, the loser's losses are cumulative—negatively.

MAKE AN ESTIMATE OF THE SITUATION—TRANSLATION

Sun Tzu continues:
When the enemy is close at hand and remains quiet, he is relying on a favorable position. When he challenges battle from afar, he

wishes to lure you to advance; when he is on easy ground, he must be in an advantageous position. When the trees are seen to move, it means the enemy is advancing; when many screens have been placed in the undergrowth, it is for the purpose of deception. The rising of birds in their flight is the sign of an ambuscade. Startled beasts indicate that a sudden attack is forthcoming.

Dust spurting upwards in high straight columns indicates the approach of chariots. When it hangs low and is widespread, it betokens that infantry is approaching. When it branches out in different directions, it shows that parties have been sent out to collect firewood. A few clouds of dust moving to and fro signify that the army is camping.

When the enemy's envoys speak in humble terms, but the army continues preparations, that means it will advance. When their language is strong and the enemy pretentiously drives forward, these may be signs that he will retreat. When light chariots first go out and take positions on the wings, it is a sign that the enemy is forming for battle. When the enemy is not in dire straits but asks for a truce, he must be plotting. When his troops march speedily and parade in formations, he is expecting to fight a decisive battle on a fixed date. When half his force advances and half retreats, he is attempting to decoy you.

When his troops lean on their weapons, they are famished. When drawers of water drink before carrying it to camp, his troops are suffering from thirst. When the enemy sees an advantage but does not advance to seize it, he is fatigued.

When birds gather above his campsites, they are unoccupied. When at night the enemy's camp is clamorous, it betokens nervousness. If there is disturbance in the camp, the general's authority is weak.

If the banners and flags are shifted about, sedition is afoot. If the officers are angry, it means that men are weary. When the enemy feeds his horses with grain, kills the beasts of burden for food and packs up the utensils used for drawing water, he shows no intention to return to his tents and is determined to fight to the death.

When the general speaks in meek and subservient tone to his subordinates, he has lost the support of his men. Too frequent rewards indicate that the general is at the end of his resources; too frequent punishments indicate that he is in dire distress. If the officers at first treat the men violently and later are fearful of them, it shows supreme lack of intelligence.

When envoys are sent with compliments in their mouths, it is a sign that the enemy wishes for a truce.

When the enemy's troops march up angrily and remain facing yours for a long time, neither joining battle nor withdrawing, the situation demands great vigilance and thorough investigation.

In war, numbers alone confer no advantage. If one does not advance by force recklessly, and is able to concentrate his military power through a correct assessment of the enemy situation and enjoys full support of his men, that would suffice. He who lacks foresight and underestimates his enemy will surely be captured by him. *

*Another translator reinforces the importance of the leader's skill in making an estimate of the situation:

There is no necessary advantage in numbers. Do not rush forward rashly, but if you calculate the forces of the enemy and then arrange your own strength accordingly you will win. But those who underrate a foe will certainly finish up as prisoners.

—A. L. Sadler

Estimate of the Situation as Used by U.S. Army Officers

1. Mission (assigned or deduced)
2. The Situation and Courses of Action

    a. Considerations affecting the Courses of Action (other operations, environment, enemy, friendly, etc.)

    b. Anticipated Difficulties

3. Analysis of Courses of Action

4. Comparison of Courses of Action

5. Decision = Commander's Concept or Intent

Questions to Determine Your Position

- What position do we own?
- What position do we want?
- Who do we have to outmaneuver?
- How much resource expenditure and time will it take?
- Can we stick it out?
- Will the results justify the expense?

Questions to Determine Your Opponent's Position

- What position do they own?
- What signals indicate they are changing or strengthening their position?
- What position do they want? (Where are they going?)
- What will the effect on us be if they are successful in their current activities?
- What opportunities will there be for us if they are unsuccessful?

MAKE AN ESTIMATE OF THE SITUATION— MANAGER'S COMMENTARY

Carefully observe the situation and attack only where real superiority can be obtained.

Amazon.com grew out of founder Jeff Bezos's personal mission to be in business for himself. His course of action was determined when he learned that books were an $82 billion market and annual growth on the web was predicted at 2,200 percent. He analyzed the opportunity for innovative computerized marketing and decided that the Seattle area would be a good hi-tech base.[1]

General Paul Cerjan, retired U.S. Army, explains how he uses the steps in conducting the Estimate of the Situation (see page 99) as a great tool for the rapid estimate of any contingency. First, you need to determine the mission. Then you start thinking what course of action you are going to take. Then you work that all the way down until you get to the decision, and from that flows the operations order—the specific orders concerning what you want done.

Depending on the circumstances, the Estimate of the Situation can be achieved rapidly or require a more lengthy analysis. We unconsciously make a rapid estimation of the situation in personal interfaces. When issuing written plans, we usually initiate an extended analysis of the situation.

I have observed real differences between the way managers from Western and Eastern civilizations gather information to make an Estimate of the Situation. The Western manager is more likely to do a quick study while the Eastern manager will often do a thorough, lengthy analysis.

There are a variety of readily perceived indicators that can help you estimate the situation. These indicators signal the competitive strategy and vulnerability. The breadth of these signals can be understood from one of Sun Tzu's translators, who identified thirty-three different signs of enemy activity by Sun Tzu in this chapter.

In personal interfaces, these indicators are called body language. Crossed arms indicate opposition. Someone leaning forward and listening indicates intent acceptance. A furrowed brow signals that your proposition is being questioned.

In business situations, the signals are also subtly visible. For example, in publicizing pricing moves, companies are signaling their desire to raise prices to others in the industry—and may reduce prices if competitors reject the signal.

All of these overt signals help the observant manager develop an accurate Estimate of the Situation. While one does not want to overestimate the opponent, it can be disastrous to underestimate.

DISCIPLINE CAN BUILD ALLEGIANCE—TRANSLATION

Sun Tzu continues:

If troops are punished before they have grown attached to you, they will be disobedient. If not obedient, it is difficult to employ them. If troops have become attached to you, but discipline is not enforced, you cannot employ them either. Thus, soldiers must be treated in the first instance with humanity, but kept under control by iron discipline. In this way, the allegiance of soldiers is assured.

If orders are consistently carried out and the troops are strictly supervised, they will be obedient. If orders are never carried out, they will be disobedient. And the smooth implementation of orders reflects harmonious relationship between the commander and his troops. *

*Other translators clarify:

If in training soldiers commands are habitually enforced, the army will be well-disciplined; if not, its discipline will be bad. If a general shows confidence in his men but always insists on his orders being obeyed, the gain will be mutual.

—Lionel Giles

If people are instructed in rules that are customary, they will be obedient, but they will not obey those to which they are not accustomed. So if it be demonstrated that the rules are customary and reliable all will be able to co-operate harmoniously.

—A. L. Sadler

The Role of Discipline

Colonel Ardant du Picq writes:

What makes the soldier capable of obedience and direction in action, is the sense of discipline. This includes: respect for and confidence in his chiefs; confidence in his comrades and fear of their reproaches if he abandons them in danger; his desire to go where others do without trembling more than they; in a word, the whole of esprit de corps. Organizations only can produce these characteristics. Four men equal a lion.

DISCIPLINE CAN BUILD ALLEGIANCE— MANAGER'S COMMENTARY

Apply the same standards to everyone.

When homerun king Henry Aaron was asked the difference between a good team and a great team, he replied promptly, "Discipline." With the discipline should come a warm concern for people.

The ideal leader is best described as one who combines excellence as a task specialist with an equal flair for the human aspects of leadership. She understands that it is people rather than techniques that really count. The manager does not have to be liked; however, she does not have to be disliked. Being fair and impartial does not mean being impersonal. At times, hard decisions must be made; when they are not made, the manager abdicates his authority.

What manager does not have his political favorites, perceived with envy by others less favored? Therein lies a complex problem: These politicians are often perceived as delivering bad information to the boss who, in turn, is perceived as delivering bad orders.

When standards for the performance of each process are established and clearly communicated, then managers can issue praise or criticism based on performance against that standard. The general manager of one of the fine hotels of the world explained to me his reason for having standards: "Maintaining known standards keeps me from playing favorites and being criticized for playing favorites." Although we find a system of standards and measures in manufacturing processes, many other office or service processes operate without clearly defined standards. Too often, where there are no standards, criticism and penalties are imposed at the whim of management. The result is confusion and low morale.

As a manager at Burger King, Herman Cain tells how he set a standard for friendly service with the "Happy B.E.E.s." The B stood for "Bad moods stay home." The Es signified, "Eye contact with customers. Everyday." This success with motivational discipline earned Cain an increase in business and a promotion up the ladder.[2]

Consistently maintaining high standards creates the environment where discipline is effective and accepted. In these circumstances, morale is high.

Personal discipline is equally important. Until a person learns how to command herself, it is unlikely that command over others will be successful.

Chapter 10

Terrain

Strategic Rules

- Know Your Battlefield
- Obey the Laws of Leadership
- Fight Only the Battles You Can Win
- Know Yourself; Know Your Opponent

Terrain is perhaps one of the most overused words in the translations of Sun Tzu. We will define "terrain" as "your area of operations"—either internal or external.

Management by wandering around the terrain is essential to success. Managers wander around not to manage, but so they can manage. By spending time at the scene of action, managers get a feel for what's happening now. Since many decisions are made at gut level, this "feel" helps process information so managers can determine a successful course of action based on real knowledge of the situation. Too often, we find decisions being made by smart people who know nothing about the circumstances.

Our bias for what we know can lead to misconceptions about the world around us. As Ralph E. Gomory, president of the Sloan Foundation, said, "We are all taught what is known, but we rarely learn about what is not known; and we almost never learn the unknowable." The point is there is a lot of information outside our area of operations. Expanding our knowledge base expands our horizon of possibilities.

Formal input systems for information are essential. However, so are informal systems such as when someone talks with his "customer"—the customer being defined as the person who receives your process.

Internally, the person who receives your process is also a customer. Within a company, people are often organized into functional departments, and these departments become competitors. Since we don't talk to competitors, there is no communication. The solution must be to achieve linkage between all processes and align them to deliver value to the ultimate customer. Until we focus all processes on the needs of the customer, the enemy will continue to be "us."

KNOW YOUR BATTLEFIELD—TRANSLATION

Sun Tzu says:

Ground may be classified according to its nature as accessible, entangling, temporizing, constricted, precipitous, and distant.

Ground which both we and the enemy can traverse with equal ease is called accessible. On such ground, he who first takes high sunny positions, and keeps his supply routes unimpeded can fight advantageously. Ground easy to reach but difficult to exit is called entangling. The nature of this ground is such that if the enemy is unprepared and you sally out, you may defeat him. But, if the enemy is prepared for your coming, and you fail to defeat him, then, return being difficult, disadvantages will ensue.

Ground equally disadvantageous for both the enemy and ourselves to enter is called temporizing. This ground is such that even though the enemy offers us an attractive bait, it will be advisable not to go forth but march off. When his force is halfway out because of our maneuvering, we can strike him with advantage. With regard to the constricted ground, if we first occupy it, we must block the narrow passes with strong garrisons and wait for the enemy. If the enemy first occupies such ground, do not attack him if the pass in his hand is fully garrisoned, but only if it is weakly garrisoned.

With regard to the precipitous ground, if we first occupy it, we must take a position on the sunny heights and await the enemy. If he first occupies such ground, we should march off and do not attack him. When the enemy is situated at a great distance from us, and the terrain where the two armies deploy is similar, it is difficult to provoke battle and unprofitable to engage him.

These are the principles relating to six different types of ground. It is the highest responsibility of the general to inquire into them with the utmost care. Conformation of the ground is of great assistance in the military operations. It is necessary for a wise general to make correct assessments of the enemy's situation to create conditions leading to victory and to calculate distances and the degree of difficulty of the terrain. He who knows these things and applies them to fighting will definitely win. He who knows them not, and, therefore, is unable to apply them, will definitely lose.

KNOW YOUR BATTLEFIELD—MANAGER'S COMMENTARY

Thorough knowledge of the scene of action is an absolute requirement.

If you were fishing in the Southwest some years ago, you might have been approached by two people of Asian descent in a pickup truck offering to clean your rod and reel. They would ask questions about your preferences in fishing equipment. Today, the Japanese are major factors in this business category.

Your "market" is those whom you must persuade to buy your product, service, or idea. The admonition to know your market may seem too basic; however, it is the basics we often miss. To know your market, you must listen to your customers. To listen effectively, you must ask questions to probe for information. This is "shut up and listen" time. Avoid defensive responses.

The big question is, "What do we need to know to make the required decision?" If we do not know what we need to know, then everything looks like important information. It becomes impossible to sort the useless from the useful.

Often, we are told what someone thinks we want to hear. Just as often, our bias from prior knowledge keeps us from finding the truth. That is why time must be spent at the scene of action finding out what's going on so we know what questions to ask.

Napoleon used both his regular army intelligence system and a focused intelligence telescope of select senior officers to gather information. Senior officers were given wide latitude to report on "anything that might interest me." Junior officers in his regular intelligence system were sent on more specific missions. He deliberately kept his telescope staff small in order to establish personal contact with these messengers. The personal contact helped him evaluate the information he received.

This focused telescope overcomes the common problem of intelligence bureaucracies. Too often, information that gets to the senior commanders is filtered through the chain of command and becomes less and less specific. The result is overgeneralization of information; consequently, those in command know the least about what is really happening. The manager's solution to learning how to interpret data is always to spend time face to face in the battlefield where the data was collected.

Don't shoot the messenger. The most rapid way to shell shock a business is to shell proof its managers.

OBEY THE LAWS OF LEADERSHIP—TRANSLATION

Sun Tzu continues:

There are six situations that cause an army to fail. They are: flight, insubordination, fall, collapse, disorganization, and rout. None of these disasters can be attributed to natural and geographical causes, but to the fault of the general.

Terrain conditions being equal, if a force attacks one ten times its size, the result is flight.

When the soldiers are strong and officers weak, the army is insubordinate.

When the officers are valiant and the soldiers ineffective, the army will fall.

When the higher officers are angry and insubordinate, and on encountering the enemy rush to battle on their own account from a feeling of resentment and the commander-in-chief is ignorant of their abilities, the result is collapse.

When the general is incompetent and has little authority, when his troops are mismanaged, when the relationship between the officers and men is strained, and when the troop formations are slovenly, the result is disorganization.

When a general unable to estimate the enemy's strength uses a small force to engage a larger one or weak troops to strike the strong, or fails to select shock troops for the van, the result is riot.

When any of these six situations exists, the army is on the road to defeat. It is the highest responsibility of the general that he examine them carefully.

If a general regards his men as infants, then they will march with him into the deepest valleys. He treats them as his own beloved sons and they will stand by him unto death. If, however, a general is indulgent towards his men but cannot employ them, cherishes them but cannot command them or inflict punishment on them when they violate

> the regulations, then they may be compared to spoiled children, and are useless for any practical purpose.

OBEY THE LAWS OF LEADERSHIP—MANAGER'S COMMENTARY

Winning is the responsibility of the leader.

The following characteristics define good command systems:

Decentralization: People have the authority needed to achieve objectives except those expressly forbidden. This reduces the need for detailed control and frees the time of leaders at all levels. Every leader commands his own unit; every subordinate knows from where to expect his instructions.

Freedom: To generate independence, freedom must be delegated all the way through the chain of command. The system doesn't work when middle managers become infatuated with their own power and fail to give up power as they are given more power in a decentralized command system.

Information processing: When senior managers give up control, they must also give up some information flow. If not, subordinates will spend too much time reporting to be effective. The task of senior management is not to confirm plans in detail; rather, it is to encourage greater speed.

Stability: People relationships and informal systems give stability to the structure of the command system.

Mutual trust: The interaction of long-standing relationships creates mutual trust. The replacement system that brings in new personnel should be structured to help create the familiarity that is an indispensable prerequisite of both reliability and trust.

A willingness to assume responsibility: To train people to accept responsibility, authority must be delegated. A decentralized command system leaves much to the discretion of individual commanders and puts responsibility squarely on their shoulders.

The right and duty of subordinate commanders to make decisions and carry them out: Freedom is granted to allow managers to make decisions and utilize available resources to find the best way to the objective.

Expect the unpredictable: Expect that plans will break down, that your opponent will behave in an unexpected manner, and that units will not achieve their objectives. Don't try to overcome the confusion by pausing to regroup after each breakdown. Keep everyone marching in the right direction.

Training: Every manager manages the training of his personnel. This does not mean that he conducts all sessions. It does mean that he has the basic responsibility for training.[1]

FIGHT ONLY THE BATTLES YOU CAN WIN—TRANSLATION

Sun Tzu continues:

Hence, if, in the light of the prevailing situation, fighting is sure to result in victory, then you may decide to fight * even though the sovereign has issued an order not to engage.

If fighting does not stand a good chance of victory, you need not to fight even though the sovereign has issued an order to engage.

Hence, the general who advances without coveting fame and retreats without fearing disgrace, whose only purpose is to protect his people and promote the best interests of his sovereign, is the precious jewel of the state.

*General Tao Hanzhang translates:

> . . . a superior general estimates the enemy situation, calculates distances and difficulty so as to control victory. He who fights with full knowledge of these factors is certain to win.

Initiating the Battle

There are two mental approaches to launching the attack:

1. Plan everything in detail and then start going. The D-Day invasion of Europe was one of the most thoroughly organized in history. With 175,000 troops from four countries involving over 5,000 ships, every detail was planned scientifically. The invasion was practiced for months in various venues around England. During the run up to the invasion, the Allies created various deceptions about where and when the invasion would occur. These were so successful that for the first hours of June 6, 1944, as troops scrambled across the beaches of Normandy, Hitler refused to believe this was the long-awaited invasion.

2. Lay down general objectives only and start immediately. The offensive is launched with the understanding that forward movement will proceed according to local circumstances. The details are filled in as the attack gains momentum. This system is used by the Israeli Defense Force.[2]

It would seem the choice is either to do it now or spend time preparing to do it later. How difficult it is to achieve the careful balance between getting ready and getting going. The best odds for success lie on the side of action. Most often, the person who does something has the best opportunity to become master of the situation.

FIGHT ONLY THE BATTLES YOU CAN WIN— MANAGER'S COMMENTARY

First understand the situation, then determine whether to fight and how.

Every executive encounters the decision of where and how to expend energy in two primary areas: the political arena and performance of her assigned tasks (either internal or external, depending on job function).

The political battles can be the most time consuming and debilitating. The larger the organization, the bigger is the political morass. Halberstam explains one type of dysfunction in his description of conflict at Ford Motor Company in *The Reckoning:*

The growing power of the finance people made the creative people more vulnerable than ever. For the creative people always, no matter how good they were, made mistakes. No product man was perfect; for every model that was a success, there were others best forgotten. By contrast, the finance men were careful. They were never identified with a particular product. They never had to create anything. In meetings they attacked but never had to defend, while the product people defended and could never attack.

In internal politics, while defending your position, target your battle against processes and systems instead of individuals. The person you attack may someday be your boss.

In determining where to fight external battles, keep your orientation focused on effectiveness. Where can you add value and win? The larger the target the bigger the results. You cannot be strong everywhere; you must determine where you are going to put your main effort and then exercise the discipline that allocates resources, directly and indirectly, to support this main effort.

If we are not effective, we have no need to be efficient. Ask Ford about its Edsel, Gerber about its failed venture into adult foods, Coca-Cola about its disastrous launch of New Coke, or the corner grocer who went out of business.

Market testing determines whether to launch a full-scale offensive. Your first objective in a test is to determine whether the concept works. Consequently, you must apply full resources to the effort. If the test fails when backed with adequate resources, you know you must abandon the effort. If it succeeds, you can adjust to make it profitable. Half-hearted tests tell you nothing.

You need to be efficient, but not at the expense of the resources needed to achieve success. An inefficient victory is bad, but not as bad as losing—which is extremely inefficient.

KNOW YOURSELF; KNOW YOUR OPPONENT—TRANSLATION

Sun Tzu says:

If we know that our troops are capable of striking the enemy, but do not know that he is invulnerable to attack, our chance of victory is but half.

If we know that the enemy is vulnerable to attack but do not know that our troops are incapable of striking him, our chance of victory is again but half.

If we know that the enemy can be attacked and that our troops are capable of attacking him, but do not realize that the conformation of the ground makes fighting impracticable, our chance of victory is once again but half.

Therefore, when those experienced in war move, they are never bewildered; when they act, they are never at a loss. Thus the saying: *Know the enemy and know yourself, and your victory will never be endangered;* * know the weather and know the ground, and your victory will then be complete.

Now, the key to military operations lies in cautiously studying the enemy's designs. Concentrate your forces in the main direction against the enemy and from a distance of a thousand li you can kill his general.

> This is called the ability to achieve one's aim in an artful and ingenious manner.

*All translations use a similar wording:

Know the enemy and know yourself and you will never be defeated.

Visible and Invisible Numbers

Even when accurate, statistics can never substitute for looking someone in the eye. Dr. W. Edwards Deming, who championed statistical quality control as a key ingredient of a quality methodology, commented that some managers look only at the visible numbers. He said, "But the visible numbers tell them so little. They know nothing of the invisible numbers. Who can put a price on a satisfied customer and who can figure out the cost of a dissatisfied customer?"

The process of stroking ourselves with our own convictions and ignoring the signals can be a spiral that ends in disaster.

KNOW YOURSELF; KNOW YOUR OPPONENT— MANAGER'S COMMENTARY

Know the strengths and weaknesses of your adversary.

When I visited the Philips office in Sao Paulo, Brazil, a senior manager told me that he employed a woman of Japanese descent as a secretary because she could read the Japanese papers ordered from Tokyo.

Communications are making the world smaller and world competitors better informed. The cost of a three-minute call from New York to London has decreased from over $200 in 1930 to about $2 today. An e-mail or Internet phone call to anywhere in the world is at no additional expense because the contact time is part of the monthly fee. For most companies, market research has expanded from domestic to world markets because we can sell to the world and the world can sell anywhere.

Countless people call on you as well as on your competitor. The editors of trade magazines know what is going on in the industry. The suppliers who call on purchasing agents know who is buying more and who is buying less—and why. Beware of the supplier who tells you everything about your competitor because he is also telling your competition about you.

Business executives who change jobs will bring their preferences in methodologies with them. They will usually clone the style of their previous organization. You can predict what they will do by where they have been. Look at both the issues and personalities. Review the issues in terms of history—who did something like this before, what happened. Look at the personalities in terms of their background of experience.

Knowledge of the personal style of competitors is the easy part; knowledge of one's self is the hard part. The higher your rank, the more difficult it is to get true feedback on your actions. Don't expect it from anyone internally. The self-examination takes place in three spheres: physical, intellectual, and moral. For physical health, see a doctor; for intellectual health, read, listen, and visit your battlefield; for moral health, find an external guru who will hold up a mirror and give you an honest picture.

Chapter 11

The Nine Varieties of Ground

Strategic Rules

- Choose a Favorable Battleground
- Shape Your Opponent's Strategy
- Make Victory the Only Option
- Plan Coordinated Efforts
- Press the Attack
- Learn Winning Ways

An ancient proverb says the first blow is as much as two; the attack has the advantage of the initiative. Since it forces action on the opponent, it relegates him to second place. The offensive action also strengthens the morale and confidence of the aggressor.

The offensive must be a continuing process. Only then does it permit you to maintain freedom of action, meet unexpected developments, and determine the future courses of action.

Tactical considerations influence strategic plans. That is, you may need to launch your offensive where it is tactically possible, not where it is strategically desirable. For example, a company with a high-end product strategy might determine that competitive success with a specific product in a mid-priced position is more readily attainable.

Two important components of the successful campaign are to strengthen customer value and know your opponent's strengths and weaknesses. In the attack, a fundamental principle is to avoid that which is strong and attack that which is weak.

While it is important to do things that give you an advantage, give serious consideration to actions that also put your competitor at a disadvantage.

The concepts of niching and segmentation provide excellent opportunities for maximizing strengths in developing offensive thrusts. Segmentation is a way for anyone of any size to secure a position by focusing strengths on a specific, narrow frontage of the market.

CHOOSE A FAVORABLE BATTLEGROUND—TRANSLATION

Sun Tzu says:

In respect to the employment of troops, ground may be classified as dispersive, frontier, key, open, focal, serious, difficult, encircled, and desperate.

When a chieftain is fighting in his own territory, he is in dispersive ground. When he has penetrated into hostile territory, but to no great distance, he is in frontier ground. Ground equally advantageous for us and the enemy to occupy is key ground. Ground equally accessible to both sides is open. Ground contiguous to three other states is focal. He who first gets control of it will gain the support of the majority of neighboring states. When an army has penetrated deep into hostile territory, leaving far behind many enemy cities and towns, it is in serious ground. Mountain forests, rugged steeps, marshes, fens, and all that is hard to traverse fall into the category of difficult ground. Ground to which access is constricted and from which we can only retire by tortuous paths so that a small number of the enemy would suffice to crush a large body of our men is encircled ground. Ground on which the army can avoid annihilation only through a desperate fight without delay is called a desperate one.

And, therefore, do not fight in dispersive ground; do not stop in the frontier borderlands.

Do not attack an enemy who has occupied key ground; in open ground, do not allow your communication to be blocked.

In focal ground, form alliances with neighboring states; in serious ground, gather in plunder.

In difficult ground, press on; in encircled ground, resort to stratagems; and in desperate ground, fight courageously.

The principle of terrain application is to make the best use of both the high and the low-lying grounds. *

*Samuel B. Griffith translates:

The tactical variations appropriate to the nine types of ground, the advantages of close or extended deployment, and the principles of human nature are matters the general must examine with the greatest care.

CHOOSE A FAVORABLE BATTLEGROUND— MANAGER'S COMMENTARY

Control of the location of the battleground results in control of offensive and defensive actions.

In retail, always be careful about attacking a competitor on its home turf. Safeway, based outside San Francisco, has a dominant market share of Northern California. It can be successfully attacked at some of its far-flung outposts. Safeway has exited major markets over its history, but it is dominant in its home market. Safeway knows their local landscape better than anyone else and has built a strong defense with relationships with local customers. There is an emotional response to defending your home market that partially transcends any ROI calculations. Any competitor looking to enter Safeway's hometown knows their likelihood of winning market share is lower, and they invest in different territories.

To discover new marketing battlefields, Pfizer organized its drug-discovery teams to pursue development of drugs for every major disease. It built speed into the process so that its drug-discovery teams needed less than one-third the industry's average person years to move a compound from conception to clinical trials. When Pfizer researchers found themselves in a race with a Japanese company for an Alzheimer's drug, they opted to drop research and form a more favorable joint venture so they could comarket the drug.

Twenty-five thousand new products are launched every year. The average forecast is that one in several hundred will succeed. Research, targeting, and luck are critical to determining where resources should be invested.

Big Island Candy in Hilo, Hawaii, selected a unique battlefield that avoids retail distribution where its product would compete with the bigger mass-marketed brands. Instead, the focus is on the tour operators who are pleased that the visit to the Big Island Candy store and factory offers an experience and products that are not available in retail stores. This marketing approach is quite immune to the moves of big competitors.

The most favorable battleground is always where you can concentrate your resources profitably with minimal competition. To control the battleground, you must offer a distinctive differentiation and the customer must desire that differentiation. Otherwise, you are another player in a low-margin commodity market.

SHAPE YOUR OPPONENT'S STRATEGY—TRANSLATION

Sun Tzu continues:

In ancient times, those described as skilled in war knew how to make it impossible for the enemy to unite his van and his rear, for his large and small divisions to cooperate, for his officers and men to support each other, and for the higher and lower levels of the enemy to establish contact with each other.

When the enemy's forces were dispersed, they prevented him from assembling them; even when assembled, they managed to throw his forces into disorder. They moved forward when it was advantageous to do so; when not advantageous, they halted.

Should one ask: "How do I cope with a well-ordered enemy host about to attack me?" I reply, "Seize something he cherishes and he will conform to your desires."

Speed is the essence of war. Take advantage of the enemy's unpreparedness, make your way by unexpected routes, and attack him where he has taken no precautions. *

*Other translators' interpretations of how your attack can shape the opponent's strategy:

In the conduct of war, speed is everything. Take the enemy unawares, follow the route unthought of by him and attack the place left ungarrisoned by him.
—Zhang Huimin

It is the nature of the army to stress speed; to take advantage of the enemy's absence; to travel unanticipated roads; and to attack when they are not alert.
—Ralph D. Sawyer

Rapidity is the essence of war; take advantage of the enemy's unreadiness, make your way by unexpected routes, and attack unguarded spots.
—Lionel Giles

SHAPE YOUR OPPONENT'S STRATEGY— MANAGER'S COMMENTARY

Move swiftly to disrupt your opponent and place him at the disadvantage.

Campbell's owns 70 percent of the canned soup business. A company called Play-By-Play dominates the carnival prize market with a 50 percent market share. Salesforce.com overshadows all competitors in the small business CRM market. Each of these companies determines the marketing situations in its industry. They own the market and their opponents must shape their attack around the strategies of these giants of their industry because the gorilla sleeps anywhere he wants.

Whether or not you can shape your opponent's strategy in business situations is a function of your relative strength. Although this relative strength is most often seen in established gorillas, new entrants with a differentiation who move rapidly can become powerful gorillas. Witness the rapid rise of Amazon.com in web marketing, Bloomberg in business information, and Staples in office products. These organizations matched differentiation with speed in order to attain strength.

You can force your opponent to react when you rapidly accumulate a critical mass of power. Napoleon said, "Force must be concentrated at one point and as soon as the breach is made, the equilibrium is broken."

In 1914, Captain Johnstone wrote that full strength is recognized as a key principle in shaping success. He said, "The best thing is to have as much as you can for yourself and as little as you can for the enemy." It is strength at a given point that shapes the opponent's reaction.

In every competitive endeavor, a concentration of energy must be rapidly achieved to attain the breakthrough. The winning manager must give priority to those items that are the most critical to success. The ultimate judge of whether you win is the customer. Her decision to buy is the critical vote. If the customer doesn't vote with a favorable decision, nothing else matters.

MAKE VICTORY THE ONLY OPTION—TRANSLATION

Sun Tzu continues:

Throw your soldiers into a position whence there is no escape, and they will choose death over desertion. For if prepared to die, how can the officers and men not exert their uttermost strength to fight? In a desperate situation, they fear nothing; when there is no way out, they stand firm. Deep in a hostile land they are bound together. If there is no help for it, they will fight hard.

Thus, without waiting to be marshaled, the soldiers will be constantly vigilant; without waiting to be asked, they will do your will; without restrictions, they will be faithful; without giving orders, they can be trusted.

Prohibit superstitious practices and do away with rumors, then nobody will flee even facing death. Our soldiers have no surplus of wealth, but it is not because they disdain riches; they have no expectation of long life, but it is not because they dislike longevity.

On the day the army is ordered out to battle, your soldiers may weep, those sitting up wetting their garments, and those lying down letting the tears run down their cheeks. But throw them into a situation where there is no escape and they will display the immortal courage of Zhuan Zhu and Cao Kuei.

He orders his troops for a decisive battle on a fixed date and cuts off their return route, as if he kicks away the ladder behind the soldiers when they have climbed up a height. When he leads his army deep into hostile territory, their momentum is trigger-released in battle. He drives his men now in one direction, then in another, like a shepherd driving a flock of sheep, and no one knows where he is going. To assemble the host of his army and bring it into danger—this may be termed the business of the general.

Set the troops to their tasks without revealing your designs. When the task is dangerous, do not tell them its advantageous aspect. Throw them into a perilous situation and they will survive; put them in desperate ground and they will live. For when the army is placed in such a situation, it can snatch victory from defeat.

MAKE VICTORY THE ONLY OPTION—MANAGER'S COMMENTARY

Lead your forces into situations where they cannot retreat.

Underlying Sun Tzu's comments is the idea that the need to survive can do much to rally everyone to achieve goals. The pressure here is of two types: personal or corporate survival.

Corporate Survival: We have seen dramatic success from a common understanding of the need for corporate survival. This was particularly true during the early days of the quality revolution when higher-quality imports threatened lower-quality domestic products. Then the rallying cry was to improve quality in order to stay in business.

Personal Survival: The threat of getting your job done right or losing it has been used by aggressive management at all levels. At companies like Pepsi, it has historically been common knowledge among managers that you make your numbers or you leave.

Competition for personal survival is also keen at the real-world management schools within corporate America such as Disney. Although renowned as a training ground for leaders, the survival process ranges from tough to brutal. For years, the Disney system pitted strong division managers against a strategic planning group that acted as a check on their power. This created inherent conflict between the groups. The best survival strategy was to fly under the radar for as long as possible.[1]

Each individual must build the kind of career strength that makes him marketable. Says Intel's Andrew Grove, "No matter where you work, you are not an employee. You are in a business with one employer—yourself—in competition with millions of similar businesses worldwide. . . . Nobody owes you a career—you own it as a sole proprietor. And the key to survival is to learn to add more value every day."[2]

With each job change or promotion, you increase your career knowledge and your value to the next employer. If you aren't moving up in your organization, then consider moving on.

In hiring people, I have always been impressed when the background indicates that one of the prior employers had a reputation for thorough screening of new hires. After selection comes training. If your company isn't training you, then you should be sending yourself to training—and that includes training inside and outside your profession.

PLAN COORDINATED EFFORTS—TRANSLATION

Sun Tzu continues:
    Troops directed by a skillful general are comparable to the Shuai Ran. The Shuai Ran is a snake found in Mount Heng. Strike at its head, and you will be attacked by its tail; strike at its tail, and you will be

attacked by its head; strike at its middle, and you will be attacked by both its head and its tail. Should one ask: "Can troops be made capable of such instantaneous coordination as the Shuai Ran?" I reply, "They can." For the men of Wu and the men of Yue are enemies, yet if they are crossing a river in the same boat and are caught by a storm, they will come to each other's assistance just as the left hand helps the right.

Hence, it is not sufficient to rely upon tethering of the horses and the burying of the chariots. The principle of military administration is to achieve a uniform level of courage.

Thus, a skillful general conducts his army just as if he were leading a single man, willy-nilly, by the hand.

The general principles applicable to an invading force are that the deeper you penetrate into hostile territory, the greater will be the solidarity of your troops, and thus the defenders cannot overcome you.

Teamwork Works

French military historian Colonel Ardant du Picq crystallized the fundamental principle underlying teamwork: "Four brave men who do not know each other well will not dare attack a lion. Four less brave, but knowing each other well, sure of their reliability and consequently of mutual aid, will attack resolutely. There is the science of organization of armies in a nutshell." There is the science of organization for teamwork in a nutshell, as well!

Colonel du Picq continues, "At any time a new invention may assure victory. Granted. But practicable weapons are not invented every day . . . the determining factor, leaving aside generals of genius, and luck, is the quality of troops, that is, the organization that best assures their esprit, their reliability, their confidence, their unity."[3]

PLAN COORDINATED EFFORTS—MANAGER'S COMMENTARY

A united effort has strength.

There are many different ways to coordinate efforts. Coca-Cola has focused on making its worldwide bottling operations more cohesive by building its strength around its larger, stronger partners.

Acquisition is another approach to obtaining a stronger united effort. The most effective acquisitions are "bolt ons" to existing core strengths. When Disney bought Marvel comics for $4 billion, purchasing Marvel's 5,000 comic book characters, the company acquired an asset that could easily add value to its existing business—movies, animation, and theme parks.

Many holding companies have reorganized and decentralized in the past decade to improve shareholder value by increasing the accountability and ownership of key business segments. Sara Lee divested several business units into freestanding companies (Coach, Hanes).

Successful companies spend a lot of time forming small teams with the mobility to maneuver. Illinois Tool Works operates through 365 small, decentralized business units that actively practice teamwork with customers and suppliers. Some may think it is inefficient to break the unit into small groups. So is defeat.

Two-time Baldrige winner Solectron is just one of many who have saved billions of dollars with teams focused on process improvement. To achieve this kind of savings, organizations have invested in training people in quality management and teamwork skills. Trained team facilitators are used to enhance team performance.

Forming effective teams takes time and training. The most successful teams are those with the best training and leadership. Successful strategic decisions are most likely to be made by teams that promote active and broad conflict over issues without sacrificing speed. The key to doing so is to mitigate interpersonal conflict. Too often, the absence of conflict is not harmony, it's apathy.[7]

When people are empowered and trained to work effectively in teams, they take ownership of the task, and the entire management process moves from control to commitment.

The team structure must be cascaded throughout the organization. Teamwork is only successful when it is led from the top. When the senior management staff functions as a team, the stage is set for all other units to operate as teams.

PRESS THE ATTACK—TRANSLATION

Sun Tzu continues:

Plunder fertile country to supply your army with plentiful food. Pay attention to the soldiers' well-being and do not fatigue them. Try to keep them in high spirits and conserve their energy. Keep the army moving and devise unfathomable plans.

It is the business of a general to be quiet and thus ensure depth in deliberation; impartial and upright, and thus keep a good management.

He should be able to mystify his officers and men by false reports and appearances, and thus keep them in total ignorance. He changes his arrangements and alters his plans in order to make others unable to see through his strategies. He shifts his campsites and undertakes marches by devious routes so as to make it impossible for others to anticipate his objective.

The different measures appropriate to the nine varieties of ground and the expediency of advance or withdrawal in accordance with circumstances and the fundamental laws of human nature are matters that must be studied carefully by a general.

Generally, when invading a hostile territory, the deeper the troops penetrate, the more cohesive they will be; penetrating only a short way causes dispersion.

> When you leave your own country behind, and take your army across neighboring territory, you find yourself on critical ground.
>
> When there are means of communication on all four sides, it is focal ground.
>
> When you penetrate deeply into a country, it is serious ground.
>
> When you penetrate but a little way, it is frontier ground.
>
> When you have the enemy's strongholds on your rear, and narrow passes in front, it is encircled ground. When there is no place of refuge at all, it is desperate ground.

PRESS THE ATTACK—MANAGER'S COMMENTARY

Keep the pressure on.

The success of organizations like Southwest Airlines and Nordstrom was not achieved with a single thrust; instead, they kept pressing the attack as they invaded each successive market.

Southwest Airlines developed systems for turning around planes faster and having crews perform multiple tasks. It kept costs low and innovated low-priced fare structures. Today, Southwest and its successful imitators (like Jet Blue) are continuing to remake the domestic airline business, driving consolidations at legacy carriers and taking prices down with each new market they enter.

Nordstrom developed a customer service philosophy and high-end brand presentation that has made it the envy of the department store industry. In an industry where it is difficult to find a clerk to take your money, Nordstrom made customer service a hallmark. While new discount stores flourish with low-end products, Nordstrom continues its offensive of high quality and value merchandise.

Several key ingredients are common to all growing organizations:

Customer focus: It matters not whether you are in a high-end business category like Nordstrom or more value oriented like Southwest; both are rated high by customers because they have created systems that deliver perceived value.

Selection: The most important contributor to the success of any organization is the ability to hire good people. I spent hours interviewing Phillip Fulmer, head football coach at the University of Tennessee, as I assisted with his book Legacy of Winning. Fulmer had one of the top winning records in college football and as such attracted good people. However, he didn't sit around waiting for them to knock on the door; he had a well-organized, systematic campaign to analyze candidates and encourage the best to sign up on his team.

Training: Hiring good people alone is not enough. Whether coaching a sports team or leading a business venture, you must be able to train the unit to be the very best. Extensive training on an ongoing basis is the hallmark of premier organizations where learning sessions are highly interactive.

The pressure necessary for success is applied by good people working within good systems that empower them to use their skills.

LEARN WINNING WAYS—TRANSLATION

Sun Tzu continues:
Therefore, in dispersive ground, I would unify the determination of the army. In frontier ground, I would keep my forces closely linked. In key ground, I would hasten up my rear elements. In open ground, I would pay close attention to my defense. In focal ground, I would consolidate my alliances. In serious ground, I would ensure a continuous

flow of provisions. In difficult ground, I would press on over the road. In encircled ground, I would block the points of access and egress. In desperate ground, I would make it evident that there is no chance of survival. For it is the nature of soldiers to resist when surrounded, to fight hard when there is no alternative, and to follow commands implicitly when they have fallen into danger.

One ignorant of the designs of neighboring states cannot enter into alliance with them; if ignorant of the conditions of mountains, forests, dangerous defiles, swamps, and marshes, he cannot conduct the march of an army; if he fails to make use of native guides, he cannot gain the advantages of the ground.

An army does not deserve the title of the invincible Army of the Hegemonic King if its commander is ignorant of even one of these nine varieties of ground. Now, when such an invincible army attacks a powerful state, it makes it impossible for the enemy to assemble his forces. It overawes the enemy and prevents his allies from joining him. It follows that one does not need to seek alliances with other neighboring states, nor is there any need to foster the power of other states, but only to *pursue one's own strategic designs to overawe his enemy. Then one can take the enemy's cities and overthrow the enemy's state.* *

Bestow rewards irrespective of customary practice and issue orders irrespective of convention and you can command a whole army as though it were but one man.

---

*Roger Ames translates:

> If you pursue you own program, and bring your prestige
> and influence to bear on the enemy, you can take his
> walled cities and lay waste to his state.

LEARN WINNING WAYS—MANAGER'S COMMENTARY

Problems are opportunities.

Winning companies are always on the offensive: Dell with new products and new markets overseas, Nucor Steel with the lowest labor cost per ton, and Wal-Mart with its ever-expanding international network of new stores.

Here are a few fundamental characteristics of winners:

Fight the battles that count: While you should not fight political battles you cannot win, when you win political battles and make enemies, you run the risk of becoming weaker. In too many cases, qualified, active people are not promoted because they have made enemies. When you can win and retain good relationships, only then can you become strong.

Avoid the avoidable: The process of avoiding the avoidable is understanding that physical hazards are identifiable obstacles against which specific measures can be taken. In contrast, the human element is completely unpredictable. Take specific actions to reduce the possibility of defeat as a result of physical conditions. This lets you devote full resources to dealing with unpredictable human elements.

Every document you present has both form and substance. You must go for the ultimate quality in the physical element of form so it doesn't detract from the more psychological elements of substance.

Considering the fragility of the human element, leave all possibilities for controllable physical mistakes to your opponent and organize for minimum physical defects in your operation. Do not allow your plan to fail because of the quality of the product or the delivery time or any physical element. The organization for excellence does not require that headquarters assumes control of everything—often decentralization is the best way to avoid physical problems.

Communicate expectations; reward achievements: Everyone must understand performance expectations in terms of specific, identifiable goals and rewards. People respond in relation to the way they are measured and rewarded.

Use a written charter to assign tasks to a team and establish boundaries. The team develops a mission statement and reconciles it with the chartering authority. Hold a celebration when results are achieved.

Set high goals: The way to consistently hit your target is to plan to achieve beyond the target. Then when you fall short, you will probably hit your goal.

Chapter 12

Attack by Fire

Strategic Rules

- Be Disruptive and Intrusive
- Consolidate Your Gains
- Exercise Restraint

People who concentrate all of their efforts on tactical issues only are working short term. They will eventually be overwhelmed by those who are doing the right thing today as part of a longer-term strategic plan. We can find the overemphasis on tactics in those who work in the more tactical selling and advertising areas of business. The overly tactical salesperson is characterized by one who concentrates only on the immediate sale and not on the long-term selling and service relationship with the customer. Overly tactical advertising concentrates on low prices without considering the debilitating effects of too much price advertising. There's an admonition: "People don't buy price; they are sold price."

The right long-term strategy can be in conflict with the need for immediate results. While a particular strategic approach may appear conceptually sound, the organization may deplete its resources before the plan yields results.

Battles can be won with tactics; however, long-range business victory comes only with the proper balance of strategy and tactics. Strategic results can be achieved only with the right mix of thinking and doing.

The offensive military commander has always known that breakthroughs are opportunities that must be exploited. Somehow, this simple truth often gets lost in the bureaucracy of organizations.

For organizations to change, the culture must change. One of the most difficult tasks facing managers who want to initiate change is how to overcome the ghosts of past corporate cultures. Even when senior managers let go of control and try to decentralize, they find scores of subordinates patiently waiting for instructions or authority. Leaders who want to reshape organizational culture must continually and actively reinforce the messages they want to deliver.

BE DISRUPTIVE AND INTRUSIVE—TRANSLATION

Sun Tzu says:

There are five ways of attacking with fire. The first is to burn soldiers in their camp; the second, to burn provision and stores; the third, to burn baggage-trains; the fourth, to burn arsenals and magazines; and the fifth, to burn the lines of transportation.

To use fire, some medium must be relied upon. Materials for setting fire must always be at hand. There are suitable seasons to attack with fire, and special days for starting a conflagration. The suitable seasons are when the weather is very dry; the special days are those when the moon is in the constellations of the Sieve, the Wall, the Wing or the Cross-bar; for when the moon is in these positions there are likely to be strong winds all day long.

Now, in attacking with fire, one must respond to the five changing situations: When fire breaks out in the enemy's camp, immediately coordinate your action from without. If there is an outbreak of fire, but the enemy's soldiers remain calm, bide your time and do not attack. When the force of the flames has reached its height, follow it up with an attack, if that is practicable; if not, stay where you are. If fires can

> be raised from outside the enemy's camps, it is not necessary to wait until they are started inside. Attack with fire only when the moment is suitable. If the fire starts from up-wind, do not launch attack from down-wind. When the wind continues blowing during the day, then it is likely to die down at night.
>
> Now, the army must know the five different fire-attack situations and wait for appropriate times.
>
> *Those who use fire to assist their attacks can achieve tangible results; those who use inundations can make their attacks more powerful.** Water can intercept and isolate an enemy, but cannot deprive him of the supplies or equipment.

*Thomas Cleary translates:

> The use of fire to help an attack means clarity;
> the use of water to help an attack means strength.

BE DISRUPTIVE AND INTRUSIVE—MANAGER'S COMMENTARY

Disrupt the mind and intrude into that disruption.

The Swatch Watch brand initially launched itself in Germany with a fully functioning 150-yard-long watch on the side of a prominent bank building in Frankfurt. When I wanted to emphasize a profit opportunity in software, I arranged for $1 million in one-dollar bills to be stacked in a giant 20-foot high display at a trade show. When FedEx launched its Saturday delivery service it sent 30,000 coffee cakes to FedEx customers—delivered by FedEx, of course.

Every commander in battle strives to achieve the breakthrough. In business, too often the search is confined to the need for sheer numbers to achieve the breakthrough. As we increase our efforts, so do our opponents. After each failure to achieve the breakthrough, the reaction is to call for a little more effort.

When we wish for just a little more time, more funds, more prospects, or more customers, we fail to realize that "just a little more" is not enough. While one company may be planning for just a little more, a competitor may be focusing on achieving a lot more. Guess who wins? Expect unexpected competition and organize for extraordinary achievements.

When we are successful in the attack, it is because of a carefully planned, extraordinary effort. Military leaders say that in order to achieve a breakthrough, two major events must happen:

1. **Dislocation:** You cannot hit the enemy unless you have first created the opportunity.
2. **Exploitation:** You cannot make that effect decisive unless you exploit the opportunity before he can recover.

The business equivalent to dislocation and exploitation is to be "disruptive" and "intrusive." You must disrupt the mind and intrude into that disruption.

Disruptive and intrusive communications have been achieved in a variety of ways. The activity ranges from the unexpected appearance of the boss at an employee event to the publicity stunt that achieves worldwide coverage.

Neither the disruption nor the intrusion that creates attention should be crass or offensive. If the disruption puts people in a negative frame of mind, the strategy backfires. To be effective, the intrusion must be directly related to your message.

CONSOLIDATE YOUR GAINS—TRANSLATION

Sun Tzu continues:

Now, to win battles and capture lands and cities but to fail to consolidate these achievements is ominous and may be described as a waste of resources and time. And, therefore, the enlightened rulers must deliberate upon the plans to go to battle, and good generals carefully execute them.*

*Here are different interpretations of Sun Tzu's words:

Unhappy is the fate of one who tries to win his battles and succeed in his attacks without cultivating the spirit of enterprise: for the result is a waste of time and general stagnation. Hence the saying: The enlightened ruler lays his plans well ahead; the good general cultivates his resources.

—James Clavell

When battles gain victories and attacks achieve occupations, yet these successes are not followed up, it is disastrous. This is known as "persisting turmoil." So an enlightened lord considers these and distinguished commanders follow them.

—J. H. Huang

CONSOLIDATE YOUR GAINS—MANAGER'S COMMENTARY

Develop sustainable loyalty.

Your objective is not just to win; your objective must be to sustain victory. When the values of the organization focus on rewarding and motivating all stakeholders, continued victory is assured.

Make the sale and lose the customer and you lose the war. In any endeavor, the highest cost is the first sale. Earning that sale is only the basis for future relationships.

The sales manager of one of the world's largest container manufacturers told me he could attribute 58 percent of his business to long-term partnering arrangements. In each instance, his company served as the sole or primary supplier to the customer. Business partnerships between customers and suppliers have become an excellent way to convert a series of transactions into a lasting relationship.

Loyalty programs that reward repeat customers are another way to develop continuing relationships. Winning is not achieved in completing one transaction; victory is in the value of multiple purchases over time. Customer loyalty is earned by those organizations that "delight" the customer. That is, these companies do not just make a sale; they satisfy the customer in such an overwhelming manner that a long-term relationship is established. Considerable evidence exists that repeat customers spend more money and are more profitable. The lifelong value of a customer at a gas station accumulates into revenue of tens of thousands of dollars and at an automobile dealership into hundreds of thousands of dollars.

Strong leaders understand that employee loyalty is as important as customer loyalty. At Hewlett-Packard, when Lewis Platt's wife died, he was thrust into the role of a single parent. When Platt reached the chief executive's position, he found that women employees were leaving in droves. Platt developed a new workplace strategy that actively encouraged employees to adjust their workweeks to meet personal responsibilities. In a memo to employees, Platt stated, "Attention to work/life issues strengthens HP's competitive edge and improves teamwork." When Platt moved up to chairman, his replacement became the third woman to head a *Fortune* 500 company.

EXERCISE RESTRAINT—TRANSLATION

Sun Tzu continues:

If not in the interests of the state, do not act. If you are not sure of success, do not use troops. If you are not in danger, do not fight a battle. *

A sovereign should not launch a war simply out of anger, nor should a general fight a war simply out of resentment. Take action if it is to your advantage; cancel the action if it is not. An angered man can be happy again, just as a resentful one can feel pleased again, but a state that has perished can never revive, nor can a dead man be brought back to life.

Therefore, with regard to the matter of war, the enlightened ruler is prudent, and the good general is full of caution. Thus, the state is kept secure and the army preserved.

*Other translators' interpretations of restraint apply equally to external strategies and internal politics:

Move only when it benefits you. In war you must win; in attacking, you must succeed. If it is not beneficial to the country, do not take action. If you cannot win, do not go to war. If you are not in danger, do not fight.
—Brian Bruya

If it is not advantageous, do not move. If objectives cannot be attained, do not employ the army. Unless endangered, do not engage in warfare.
—Roger Ames

No action should be taken unless it is to your advantage; no army should be committed unless you are sure of victory; no war should be waged unless you have no alternative.
—Zhang Huimin

EXERCISE RESTRAINT—MANAGER'S COMMENTARY

Do not fight battles you cannot win—or win those that lose the war.

External Restraint

Manufacturers who want to invade new foreign markets have not been very successful with the head-on attack of heavy advertising investments and massive campaigns. New markets are conquered by deliberate, skillfully executed campaigns focused on methodically out-maneuvering entrenched competitors.

Coke has a large share of the Japanese market for soft drinks because it took the time and made the investment to build a full range of functional strengths. When Coke made its first move into Japan, it found a complex, multilayered distribution system. Using local bottlers, Coke recreated the kind of sales force it uses in the United States. Instead of servicing accounts with independent wholesalers or distributors, in Japan today the Coke van replaces empty bottles with new ones. By investing heavily in resources in the distribution system, Coke redefined the domestic game in Japan. Short-term financial returns were sacrificed to achieve long-term gains.[1] Now, as it establishes itself in China, Coke is adapting this same game plan to another fast-growing market.

A different approach in the invasion of markets is to use existing distributors and/or sales representatives as the delivery system. Only after strength is achieved is the transition made to corporate distribution centers by either purchasing distribution facilities or buying out agreements. The growth of successful distribution in many industries nationally can be traced to the use of outside agents to internally controlled delivery systems.

Internal Restraint

The issue of fighting a battle you cannot win has special applications for corporate politics. Good politicians negotiate; bad politicians fight battles.

Hundreds of years before Christ, a Chinese warlord gave the following advice, which has real application for corporate politics:

> *One who gains one victory becomes the Emperor;*
> *One who gains two, a King;*
> *One who gains three, Lord Protector;*
> *One who gains four is exhausted;*
> *One who gains five victories suffers calamity.*

Chapter 13

Employment of Secret Agents

Strategic Rules

- Invest in Intelligence Resources
- Establish an Active Intelligence System
- Practice Counterintelligence

In many organizations, a major problem is organizing, synthesizing, and disseminating information. Most organizations are plagued with "islands of information." Many people know many things, but no system exists to put it all together for verification and application to specific objectives. Even in the CIA, most of the information is obtained from overt, not covert, sources. The biggest job for any intelligence unit is organizing and interpreting readily available information.

Uncertainty surrounds many of the issues challenging the manager. The antidote for uncertainty is more relevant information. The more information available, the longer the time needed to process it and the greater the danger of failing to distinguish between the relevant and the irrelevant.

According to General Gordon R. Sullivan, a retired army chief of staff, "The paradox of war in the Information Age is one of managing massive amounts of information and resisting the temptation to over-control it. The competitive advantage is nullified when you try to run decisions up and down the chain of command. . . . Once the commander's intent is understood, decisions must be devolved to the lowest possible level to allow these front line soldiers to exploit the opportunities that develop."[1]

Wegmans Food Markets, headquartered in upstate New York, has been described in the *Wall Street Journal* as a retailer somewhere between Nordstrom and Harrods. Wegmans's store managers regularly hold focus-group sessions with eight to ten customers to discuss their likes and dislikes. Because this front-line research is conducted by store managers with their own customers, suggestions can be immediately implemented. This is just one reason why Wegmans's average store volume is four times greater than the national average.

INVEST IN INTELLIGENCE RESOURCES—TRANSLATION

Sun Tzu says:

Generally, when an army of one hundred thousand is raised and dispatched on a distant war, the expenses borne by the people together with the disbursements made by the treasury will amount to a thousand pieces of gold per day. There will be continuous commotion both at home and abroad; people will be involved with convoys and exhausted from performing transportation services, and seven hundred thousand households will be unable to continue their farmwork.

Hostile armies confront each other for years in order to struggle for victory in a decisive battle; *yet if one who begrudges the expenditure of one-hundred pieces of gold in honors and emoluments remains ignorant of his enemy's situation, he is completely devoid of humanity.* * Such a man is no leader of the troops; no capable assistant to his sovereign; no master of victory.

*General Tao Hanzhang translates:

> If one who begrudges rank, honors, and a few hundred pieces
> of gold remains ignorant of his enemy's situation, he is
> completely unaware of the interest of the state and people.

Collect all Available Data

The first rule of data collection is stated in the army regulations of the People's Republic of China:

> *Every commander must organize reconnaissance within his unit's zone of activities. He must not wait for instructions from his superior, nor must he seek his superior's decision as to whether he should organize reconnaissance.*

The second rule of data collection is that much of what you need to know is already known. To learn what needs to be done, search your neighborhood or benchmark the world, and you will find someone who is already doing "it" successfully. Theodore Levitt says it this way: "The future doesn't descend on us on some prophetic day . . . it grows out of forces which are now turbulently in motion."

INVEST IN INTELLIGENCE RESOURCES— MANAGER'S COMMENTARY

Information is crucial to winning.

Successful ventures do good intelligence homework so they can target their products.

Accurate intelligence allows for better use of your resources. The information derived reduces risks because you have the data that gives you better odds. Only a gambler with inside information can rationally bet her whole stake on a single race. Good marketing research management puts you in the business of managing risks instead of taking risks.

The key assumption of intelligence is that an impression of what is not known can be pieced together by studying what is known. Good strategy needs good assumptions, and good assumptions are a product of good intelligence.

America's most successful corporations have large cadres of internal and external market research services. They treat marketing research as a corporate asset because it helps them market more effectively and efficiently.

It is easy to do bad market research because we so often want to ask the questions that will tell us what we want to hear. Before determining questions, you must learn everything you can about the area you want to study. That means personal visits to the places where your product or service is consumed.

Too often, we think that knowledge of ourselves and our opponent is a destination we've already reached. Gathering knowledge is an ongoing, dynamic feedback process.

Improper action from advance signals can exacerbate the problem. An abundance of information incorrectly interpreted can lead to fatally wrong conclusions.

In intelligence failures, the problem is not that the information is unavailable; rather, it is not taken seriously by commanders who, once committed to a course of action based on bureaucratic consensus, refuse to recognize the validity of contrary data and are unwilling to abandon the original operation.

You must know your opponent and understand her strengths and weaknesses. You must understand everything you can about the current and future markets for your product, service, or idea.

ESTABLISH AN ACTIVE INTELLIGENCE SYSTEM—TRANSLATION

Sun Tzu continues:

Now, the reason that the enlightened sovereign and the wise general conquer the enemy whenever they move and their achievements surpass those of ordinary men is that they have foreknowledge. This 'foreknowledge' cannot be elicited from spirits, nor from gods, nor by analogy with past events, nor by any deductive calculations. It must be obtained from the men who know the enemy situation.

Hence, the use of spies, of whom there are five sorts: native spies, internal spies, converted spies, doomed spies, and surviving spies.

When all these five sorts of spies are at work and none knows their method of operation, it would be divinely intricate and constitutes the greatest treasure of a sovereign.

Native spies are those we employ from the enemy's country people. Internal spies are enemy officials whom we employ.

Converted spies are enemy spies whom we employ.

Doomed spies are those of our own spies who are deliberately given false information and told to report it.

Surviving spies are those who return from the enemy camp to report information.

Hence, of all those in the army close to the commander, none is more intimate than the spies; of all rewards, none more liberal than those given to spies; of all matters, none is more confidential than those relating to spying operations.

He who is not sage cannot use spies. He who is not humane and generous cannot use spies. And he who is not delicate and subtle cannot get the truth out of them. Delicate indeed! Truly delicate! *

*Another translator identifies the need for the manager's wisdom in conducting research and intelligence activities:

No one but a sage can utilize espionage; except with humanity, one cannot deploy agents; except with thorough observation, one cannot gain truth from agents. Observe! Observe!
—J. H. Huang

ESTABLISH AN ACTIVE INTELLIGENCE SYSTEM— MANAGER'S COMMENTARY

Establish a methodology for processing information.

Organize Your Information Flow

The process of gathering intelligence is one of collecting and filtering. All information is not useful; too much information can make it difficult to separate the useful from the useless. One of the key decisions in processing information is how to be selective in the information flow to each level of management.

The ultimate solution is a combination of:

* Structure, which sizes the organization's decision-making process;
* Good information available at all levels;
* Personal reconnaissance on the part of decision makers at every level.

Make Information Useful

To make scattered information useful, it has to be pulled together piece by piece and developed to form distinct patterns to enlighten all echelons. This coordinating process is what makes intelligence useful. Confronted with a task and not having enough information to perform the task, an organization will either centralize or decentralize.

Centralizing keeps decision thresholds high and increases the information flow. Centralization also requires more information processing capability, thereby creating a more complex system.

Decentralizing divides the task into parts and establishes focal points to deal with each part. This relocates the decision thresholds to lower levels.[2]

Most often, the best choice will be to decentralize and segment the task into manageable parts. This requires management that is willing to accept less certainty at the top in order to have more certainty at the bottom.

Systems Are Not Solutions

Too often, managers are disappointed because they expected the new information system to provide new solutions. Battles are not won with systems; they are won with that supreme weapon—the personal factor.

Although it would seem the command structure should determine whether the information system should be centralized or decentralized, often the reverse is true. It is the ability of the system to absorb and process information that determines whether a centralized or decentralized command structure can be the most effective way to organize.

PRACTICE COUNTERINTELLIGENCE—TRANSLATION

Sun Tzu continues:

There is no place where espionage is not possible. * If plans relating to spying operations are prematurely divulged, the spy and all those to whom he spoke of them should be put to death.

Generally, whether it be armies that you wish to strike, cities that you wish to attack, and individuals that you wish to assassinate, it is necessary to find out the names of the garrison commander, the aides-de-camp, the ushers, gatekeepers, and bodyguards. You must instruct your spies to ascertain these matters in minute detail.

It is essential to seek out enemy spies who have come to conduct espionage against you and bribe them to serve you. Courteously exhort them and give your instructions, then release them back home. Thus, converted spies are recruited and used. It is through the information brought by the converted spies that native and internal spies can be recruited and employed. It is owing to their information, again, that the doomed spies, armed with false information, can be sent to convey it to the enemy. Lastly, it is by their information that the surviving spies can come back and give information as scheduled. The sovereign must have full knowledge of the activities of the five sorts of spies. And to know these depends upon the converted spies. Therefore, it is mandatory that they be treated with the utmost liberality.

In ancient times, the rise of the Shang Dynasty was due to Yi Zhi, who had served under the Xia. Likewise, the rise of the Zhou Dynasty was due to Lu Ya, who had served under the Yin. Therefore, it is only the enlightened sovereign and the wise general who are able to use the most intelligent people as spies and achieve great results. Spying operations are essential in war; upon them the army relies to make its every move.

*Ralph D. Sawyer translates:

There are no areas in which one does not employ spies.

PRACTICE COUNTERINTELLIGENCE—MANAGER'S COMMENTARY

While you get their secrets, protect your own.

You should take deliberate steps to keep competitors from learning what is going on in your business. For example, at one headquarters, a poster in the company cafeteria reminds employees that, "Loose lips sink ships." The media has run enough stories about corporate espionage to make managers aware of the danger, but constant reminders are needed.

When a smaller entrepreneur visited Japan, he found to his surprise that the practice of gathering competitive information is not confined to big companies. After a few drinks one evening, his host took him to a file cabinet and produced a file containing information about the visitor's company.

The first bastion of counterintelligence is usually a memo that requires all employees to refer outside inquiries for information to the public relations officer. This is a good practice since the stories are legion from managers who tell about making a phone call to a targeted company and learning everything they wanted to know.

At the next level of protection are security measures such as a paper shredder in key offices and numbering systems to control key documents like new product plans. Every manager should be concerned about documents on his desk in view of visitors because too many people have learned how to read upside down. The best way to handle visitors is to meet them in a separate conference room with no visible company information.

Security measures are not limited to the office. Although laptop computers are useful on an airline flight, keep in mind that the information may also be useful to a nearby passenger.

The top level of protection is active measures involving checking for bugs in telephones and making sure that rooms engaged for outside conferences are secure and no material is left behind after the meeting.

PART TWO

APPLYING SUN TZU'S WISDOM

The key issue for managers is not knowing the gems of wisdom from Sun Tzu but applying the wisdom—successfully taking action is more difficult than knowing what to do.

Practical Applications

Managers' Examples

孫子

Following are useful applications harvested from contributions by managers around the world. Each manager has her own favorite quotes. Here are the gems I often consider.

Avoiding conflict: *To subdue the enemy without fighting is the supreme excellence.* This simple concept of winning without fighting differentiates Sun Tzu from the rush to attack so prevalent in Western thinking. His central thesis is to defeat the enemy by using wisdom rather than force. He says, *"Subdue the enemy without fighting . . . capture his cities without assaulting them . . . overthrow his state without protracted operations."*

Strategic planning: *A victorious army wins its victories before seeking battle; an army destined for defeat fights in the hope of winning.* This simple wisdom emphasizes the important role of strategic planning in determining where and how you can win.

Concentration of resources: *A weak force will eventually fall captive to a stronger one . . . and . . . we can keep our forces concentrated while the enemy must be divided.* Statements like these emphasize the value of focusing strengths against weaknesses.

Achieving victory: *Use the normal force to engage; use the extraordinary to win.* Too many times plans are for the ordinary instead of the extraordinary. The idea of doing the extraordinary inspired me to display $1 million in one-dollar bills at a trade show to dramatize a million-dollar profit opportunity. We made our point. Sales and profits went off the chart.

Use of intelligence: *The reason the enlightened sovereign and wise general's achievements exceed those of ordinary men is because of fore-knowledge . . . and . . . know the enemy and know yourself, and you can fight a hundred battles with no danger of defeat.* Good intelligence is as important today as it was 2,500 years ago.

—*Gerald Michaelson*

INVEST IN INTELLIGENCE

David Rich
President and CEO, ICC/Decision Services

ICC/Decision Services works with the largest retailers on the globe to measure, manage, and improve the customer experience. ICC strongly believes that ultimately the experience is the brand. And like any great brand, it needs to be repeatable and consistent.

We are in the information services business, so when Sun Tzu speaks of employing "secret agents" to collect good intelligence, it resonates with me. Good information is critical to success, but too often we work with organizations that either don't want to acquire good information or don't know how to utilize it once they acquire it. Some common mistakes include only using one source for gathering information: a customer satisfaction survey or a focus group. These are all very good tools to have in your arsenal, but when used individually or in isolation they do not lead to success on the brand battlefield.

Another common mistake is creating silos within a company, and not sharing valuable information across divisions. When management makes intelligence a commodity, it can lead to ineffective and poor results. A fragmented approach to intelligence gathering or using intelligence punitively rather than to provide incentive to management and sales associates can adversely affect your customer experience. Ultimately, the cost of doing it wrong will be much greater than the cost of getting it right.

ICC has developed our own six-step process for intelligence gathering comprised of:

1. **Discovery:** Initiate a process for improvement in an organization and identify customers' needs (key value and service attributes).
2. **Design:** Design a survey instrument and the survey methodology.

3. **Delivery:** Conduct measurement programs and analyze the satisfaction information collected.
4. **Discourse:** All insights and findings need to be internally evaluated to determine their true impact and meaning.
5. **Direction:** Communicate the insights discovered to management and employees. Acknowledge customers' participation.
6. **Decisions:** Develop improvement plans and monitor improvement progress.

A 400-store retailer employed a full-service intelligence system that employs weekly mystery shopping at its locations, daily customer satisfaction surveys, and a rolling employee-engagement survey program to measure success. Before rolling out the program, we did employee huddles and customer exit interviews to gauge where to begin. This data was then funneled throughout the organization, and all departments worked together to develop the mystery shopping (objective measurement), customer satisfaction surveys (subjective measurement), alongside an employee engagement program. The employee engagement program is critical because if employees are not engaged it will ultimately damage the customer experience, which will be reflected in the mystery shops and/or customer satisfaction surveys. We use the process above to work the program through the organization from bottom to top and back down again, while doing cross analysis of all metrics to make sure they correlate with sales and profits. It's an active intelligence system—and one of our best weapons for producing ROI for our clients.

SKIP THE FRONTAL ASSAULT

Angelo Vassallo
Senior Vice President, Pernod-Ricard Beverages

After World War II, veterans returning to the United States returned with a taste for a popular European spirit: rum. When combined with a native American beverage, Coke, Rum and Coke became a popular beverage of the post-War boom. And the dominant brand was Bacardi.

Seagrams first tried to attack Bacardi's hold on that market with a classic frontal attack. Seagrams's first effort was a Bacardi-like rum, Ronrico. Ronrico was introduced in the seventies, and Seagrams invested heavily in its introduction, giving it a Bacardi-like flavor profile and "from the islands" imagery. Since its only advantage versus highly entrenched Bacardi was a slightly lower price, it never became a strong seller, and Bacardi continued to dominate the U.S. rum business.

Wanting to get a stronger piece of this business, Seagrams tried a different tact a few years later. Several of us working on new innovations were tasked with finding a different way into the rum business. This time, we followed Sun Tzu's stratagem to "attack by an unexpected route."

First, the group decided to offer a different flavor of rum. We experimented with different rum-flavor profiles and created one that had a slight vanilla flavor that mixed well with other beverages—particularly orange juice. Second, a brand was developed that appealed to a younger drinker. Captain Morgan—the brand name picked—was actually a small brand the company owned in Europe. That brand name was Americanized and the Captain Morgan character was made a younger and more pronounced character.

And finally, a group hungry to introduce the brand was identified—the Calvert's organization, traditionally only given niche or tired brands to sell, brands that were too small for the other divisions to handle. The group was given the product and challenged to show what they could do with it. Captain Morgan became a success.

After performing a variety of roles in different countries, years later I came back to a job that had this U.S. brand as part of my group. It had grown for a few years, and the owner of Seagrams challenged me to grow it even further, giving me two weeks to come back to him with a plan.

That plan took Captain Morgan to its next level of success. In a move few brands had made, we lowered the proof of the product 10 points. Spirits are taxed based on proof content, so that move lowered the tax per bottle by $4. We also raised the price $5. We proposed significantly increasing the value of the product to our company—increasing the per-case profits by over 50 percent through those two actions. The result? The younger drinking consumer did not miss the alcohol and did not think the price increase was excessive. The first year we sold the same number of units as the prior year and profits went through the roof, giving us the margins to invest more in that brand. Captain Morgan has been a continual success ever since and today is the preferred rum amongst the over-twenty-one consumer.

BUILD ON STRENGTHS, ATTACK WEAKNESSES

Jeff Tripician
CMO/EVP Niman Ranch

As one of the premier niche Gourmet brands in the country in 2006, Niman Ranch had developed a truly unique live-side supply network consisting of over 400 U.S. family hog, cattle, and lamb farmers. This network of farmers produced a superior-tasting product, but suffered from inconsistency in quality from farm to farm due to the number of independent farms involved.

The company operated out of Oakland, CA and from there ran a meat distribution facility that cut meat and managed delivery routes, food service sales, retail sales, internet sales, feedlot operations, and farmer auditing. As a result, the company was overextended in its scope of business and geographically constricted, with over 80 percent of its business route within truck-driving distance of its Oakland plant.

After our acquisition of Niman in August of 2006, the company developed a more strategically focused business model built around its two core competencies: live-side procurement and branded sales and marketing. This leveraged the quality and the mystique of the brand name—two advantages larger national competitors could not easily emulate. As Sun Tzu advises, "That you are certain to take what you attack is because you attack a place the enemy does not or cannot protect."

The company closed the Oakland plant (stopped cutting and distributing meat) and switched to a distributor system. Niman established a centralized distribution hub in Iowa for all customer orders in order to efficiently supply all distributors nationally via one consolidated order for all Niman Ranch products (beef, pork, lamb, poultry, processed products).

The company developed a national retail and food service distribution network of over forty companies that would distribute Niman Ranch meats within their market area, using their trucks and their sales force. The change in Niman's business model allowed the company to focus on growing its live-side farmer network from 400 farmers to over 650—dramatically increasing supply and supporting the growth. It allowed the company to hone the live-side protocols for raising livestock, increasing the consistency and quality of the product. On the sales and marketing side, the new business model allowed the company to double in size over the same time period and increase gross margin by targeting the top customers in each market to carry and brand the product line on their menus and in their stores.

The brand is now on over 5,000 menus nationally and placed in niche/specialty grocery stores from Maine to Miami and Seattle to San Diego.

A MARINE OFFICER'S VIEWPOINT

Bruce M. MacLaren
Colonel, U.S. Marine Corps (Ret.)

I have always had Sun Tzu's *The Art of War* close at hand, especially during my thirty years as an officer of Marines. In 1953 when I was a cadet at Norwich University, Major General Harmon (Ret.) suggested that all cadets should start reading the Master's treatise as well as Clausewitz. His reasoning was that our nation was becoming more involved in unconventional conflicts. The Korean War focused my attention on General Harmon's suggestion. In 1954, as a new officer in the Marine Corps, my basic training company commander reiterated that all hands should make *The Art of War* required professional reading. In 1963, Brigadier General Samuel B. Griffith U.S.M.C. (Ret.) translated his version of *The Art of War*. He also translated Mao's *Chinese Guerrilla Warfare*.

Both of these treatises became pocket manuals in the field as well as in training during peacetime as far as I was concerned—especially during my many years of service in the Far East. Knowledge of *The Art of War* became a professional link between myself and other foreign officers, especially the Chinese, Korean, Thai, and Vietnamese. I recall many times in Vietnam where our major units would overreact to enemy efforts in the East, only to be struck unaware in the West. Reading Sun Tzu conditioned me to put myself into my enemy's thought process and to better anticipate events. It slowed me down and stimulated my own thought process—probably saving my life.

Even after retirement, I was able to apply the lessons of Sun Tzu in local civic endeavors to keep our town great. Also, as a middle school teacher in social studies, I imparted some of *The Art of War* theories to the best of the brightest who were headed to high school and on to college and corporate endeavors. Michaelson's great book, *Winning the Marketing War,* is still used. The local high school now has its own copy. I must add that Confucius's analysis was better received by some of my less-than-dynamic middle-school students.

Militarily, I favor *The Art of War* translations of General Samuel Griffith, Thomas Cleary, and my old Chinese friend and mentor, Major General Tao Hanzhang P.L.A. (Ret.), whose input helped me earn a degree at the University of Maine. As far as applying *The Art of War* to the business world, Michaelson's work is that of a master! Those who read his advice as they enter the world of competitive business will win their corporate battles; those who don't will fall by the wayside.

SEIZE A MEANINGFUL ADVANTAGE

Peter Brennan
Retired President, Daymon Associates

Daymon Worldwide has a reputation as private-label experts throughout the world. Currently, the company represents over 5,000 suppliers in twenty-four countries and has over 5,000 employees. This private-label expertise developed over a forty-year history, through the development of insightful relationships with retail customers in hundreds of locations.

One of the early strategies of the organization was to dedicate teams of people to operate at each retail customer location and help develop a unique relationship with the end consumer. In part because of their location, these dedicated teams of associates working with individual customers evolved to become experts in the individual objectives and goals of those customers. Sun Tzu says, "Nothing is more difficult than the art of maneuvering for seizing favorable positions beforehand," and our strategy accomplished that. Our company headquarters became an intelligence center where more knowledge developed with universal applications to most areas of the business.

Our growth was affected by increasingly competent managers at the local level who were empowered to give headquarters input regarding support they needed. In turn, we could quickly develop systems and solutions needed immediately in the marketplace. These strong and savvy local entrepreneurs became a communication system to bring what was needed in the local markets to the headquarters and for us to be able to see emerging trends long before they became broadly accepted.

Throughout the history of our company, we have been faced with consolidation in the retail industry. This consolidation of retailers has necessitated appealing to a new corporate entity who acquired a successful customer with whom we had a relationship. In doing so, we have frequently faced competitors who had a pre-existing relationship with the consolidator. Our future became dependent upon demonstrating we had more to offer than the competitor with whom the surviving client had a long-term relationship. Thus, every consolidation scenario commenced with a complete diagnostic of what we needed to accomplish offensively at the larger customer. Or, as Sun Tzu would advise, that "the enlightened sovereign and the wise general conquer the enemy whenever they move and their achievements surpass that of ordinary men in that they have foreknowledge." Recognizing our former customer no longer existed and was now part of a larger entity was critical in this thought process. Consolidation in and of itself creates new complications for customer and supplier alike, and we were able to change our strategy from what it had been to servicing a far more complex, diverse organization. This normally made us the preferred choice when our customer was part of a consolidation.

REORGANIZING THE BATTLEFIELD

Jay Kurtz

President, KappaWest

Laguna Hills, California

Background: As a student at Canada's Royal Military College, I became familiar with Sun Tzu. As a business consultant, I used the principles of Sun Tzu and other great captains to aid our clients. Here is an example.

Situation: State Bell (not its real name) is a regional telephone company operating in a remote area. The state public utility commission wanted to increase competition and advised State Bell that it expected the company to give up significant market share. New generations of technology were emerging and competition was invading. To satisfy the regulators and incur minimum impact to State Bell, we heeded Sun Tzu's advice: *Enlightened rulers must deliberate upon the plans to go to battle, and good generals carefully execute them.*

Strategy: Sun Tzu says, *Wise generals win because they have foreknowledge.* State Bell undertook a market study and classified customers as:

- **Green**—would very likely stay with State Bell
- **Amber**—would not actively seek a competitive system, but would seriously consider another company's proposal
- **Red**—would aggressively look for a competitor to replace State Bell

State Bell persuaded the utility commission to define the reduction in terms of number of customers instead of number of lines. It then redefined the market using Sun Tzu's advice to *make use of both the high and low-lying grounds.* "High ground" was customers with the greater number of lines. The "swamps" were smaller red and amber customers with fewer lines and lower revenue.

Implementation: We organized around Sun Tzu's wisdom: *By taking into account the favorable factors, he makes his plan feasible.* State Bell trained a team of sales personnel to convert the larger amber customers with more lines to the newest generation of technology. They also sought longer leases with large customers. In its strategic withdrawal, State Bell allowed competitors to "capture" smaller customers with fewer lines. Consequently, it did not allow any competitor to achieve the critical mass that would justify a full-time service center in any area. This gave State Bell an important service quality superiority.

Results: State Bell lost enough customers—30 percent—to satisfy the utility commission's measure of customers. State Bell won this battle by keeping the bigger customers so that it lost only 15 percent of its lines and revenue.

WIN WITHOUT FIGHTING

Gregg A. Nathanson

Manager, Real Estate Practice Group,

Couzens, Lansky, Fealk, Ellis, Roeder & Lazar

The Art of War speaks to sophisticated, twenty-first-century transactional real estate law practice.

Consider Sun Tzu's central thesis that you can avoid fighting when you plan the right strategy before the battle. Strategy, Sun Tzu teaches, is the planning process, the war on paper. Tactics, in contrast, implement the plan. Tactics are the contract process, the battle.

Every smooth, successful real estate transaction is won or lost in the planning process. An artful purchase agreement bridges strategy and tactics. The buyer wants the seller's property; the seller wants the buyer's money. That is the essence of the relationship. With a well-crafted purchase agreement, each side's rights and duties are clearly defined. The essential elements of closing the transaction have been predetermined. So, the ultimate tactical point of contact, the closing, goes smoothly. Conflict and fighting are avoided because the parties planned the right strategies at the beginning of the transaction.

Sometimes, a transaction does not pursue the smooth course anticipated by the purchase agreement. With today's depressed real estate economy, many property owners are "underwater," and have negative equity. Many property owners with negative equity engage in a "short sale." The mortgage lender agrees to release their lien on the property and come up "short" by accepting less than the full amount due.

In one recent transaction, we represented a homeowner with two lenders. We fought to convince each of them to accept a short sale. This was not your ordinary residential transaction; the amount of debt exceeded $1,000,000. We employed varied tactics with each point of contact—the individuals representing the lenders. Ultimately, we were successful in helping our client achieve victory by liquidating their underwater asset and walking away from two sizeable potential deficiency judgments. To a lesser extent, each of the secured lenders achieved a victory as well, since they received more money by compromising and permitting the transaction to close than they would have received otherwise.

In this scenario, flexibility and maneuvering were key—the value of the property was already a loss to each side's original expectations. Sun Tzu advises, "If equally matched, be capable of dividing him, if less in number, be capable of defending yourself." Since there was more the lenders could have lost, the seller, with our help, was able to defend himself.

FAVORITE APPLICATIONS

John Shamley
Program Director, Compensation
Federal Aviation Administration

When I took my first Chinese history course, I never dreamed I would become a Chinese history major and that Chinese philosophy would be so important to my life. The teachings of Sun Tzu in *The Art of War* are special.

Upon entering the business world, I learned that Sun Tzu had applications I did not recognize as a student. It was particularly relevant to recognize that Sun Tzu's work deals with human beings and their endeavors. Here are a few applications I have found useful.

Be Flexible: My favorite quote is: *Hence no one victory is gained in the same manner as another*. Often in government, we rush to find the "model" or "formula" that makes experience and reasoned judgment unnecessary. What folly! One size does not fit all situations, and we must be flexible in customizing systems to the situation.

Do Not Attack Head-On: *What is difficult is to make a devious route the most direct and to turn disadvantage into advantage*. What Sun Tzu is saying is we can avoid conflict in solving problems by not using the direct approach. In organizations that did not recognize the need for change, I have seen people eaten alive when they tried to initiate change head-on.

Strength Against Weakness: *His offensive will be irresistible if he plunges in the enemy's weak points*. In our organization, we found the weakness was intense resistance to change. We recognized that the enemy was us, so we attacked our own weakness and developed innovative and creative responses to change.

Take the Initiative: *A good commander creates a posture releasing an irresistible and overwhelming momentum.* A new compensation initiative had a positive effect on awakening our organizational inertia.

People Are a Valuable Asset: *He treats them as his own beloved sons and they will stand by him until death.* When we treat people as people, the increase in morale and performance cannot be overstated.

Warning: When using the wisdom of Sun Tzu, you will be more successful if you do not overtly state the principles being utilized.

SUN TZU IN THE BOARDROOM

Domminick Attanosio
Senior Adviser, Young and Partners LLC
New York, New York

Some years ago, I served on the board of a public pharmaceutical company that was developing a new delivery system to provide adjustable dosing of oral medications. The product targeted the pediatric and geriatric markets. I suggested the board consider the following precepts of Master Sun Tzu in their deliberations.

Know the enemy and know yourself, and you can fight 100 battles with no danger of defeat. To better know our competitors, we developed a system that monitored the drug industry to track emerging technologies that could impact our dosing system. To ensure our own strength, we engaged the services of the best marketing research and development engineering people we could find.

Travel where there is no enemy. Since the smaller segments of the pediatric and geriatric markets were given limited attention by potential competitors, we guided development efforts into these smaller segments.

Pursue one's strategic designs to overawe the enemy. There were many financial temptations to deviate from our decided mission. We passed by potential investor windfalls in favor of maintaining our long-term objectives.

An army can be raised only when the money is in hand. Authorizing the balance of finances in product development with investor relations, we fulfilled the board's fiduciary responsibility for this emerging public company to assure the timely development of technology with adequate funding for the venture.

The general whose only interest is to protect his people and promote the best interests of his sovereign is the precious jewel of the state. We ensured that our senior managers had proven track records in their respective jobs and adjusted organizational responsibilities accordingly.

The enlightened rulers must deliberate upon the plans to go to battle, and good generals carefully execute them. The statutory responsibility of the board was to keep the company on the offensive with the appropriate management team.

We believed in the philosophy that makes Sun Tzu unique: *To subdue the enemy without fighting is the supreme excellence.* Providing the public with needed technology enabled the board to guide the company to its ultimate victory.

The final chapter in the company's successful history was written when the organization was purchased and stockholders earned an equitable return on their investment.

TAKE THE INITIATIVE

Stan Johnson
President, Johnson&Company

Johnson&Company is a boutique human resources firm located in Connecticut. We offer executive search services as well as a range of organizational consulting. From the start, I positioned this business not just as an executive search, but as a full human resources partner for clients looking to build or optimize leadership teams. This differentiated view of partnering with our clients and immersing ourselves in their organization to provide executive search and related services has worked well.

I started Johnson&Company in the recession of the early nineties. Starting a new business like this in the midst of a recession may seem like bad timing; however, I reasoned there was a very large demand for executive search that included looking at how a client's organization would have to be configured when the economy turned and an equal demand to fill holes in top management's skill set. Even in a recession where my category was cut in half, the demand for executive search would still be very large—many hundreds of millions of dollars. I just needed to get my piece of it. And since my intent was to be a boutique firm, I only needed to get a modest-sized piece.

As Sun Tzu advises, "Know the enemy and know yourself and your victory will never be endangered." I knew the competitive landscape from my time as the senior partner of one of the largest executive search firms, so I also knew where a smaller company could find success, since we would have very few client or candidate conflicts and I would be involved in every engagement.

Since then I have built a steady business. Even in the most recent, and deeper recession, my business has been very strong. There are a couple of ways I have been able to do this:

I am fortunate to have come out of one of the great executive training schools—Procter and Gamble. During my time there and in the executive search firm, I had a chance to build relationships with successful business leaders at many of our largest corporations—decision makers for the kinds of services Johnson&Company offers.

I have built the business on strong service and long-term successes—word of mouth has been my best advertising and my clients are the people, not the corporations. When they moved, I went with them.

While I continue to successfully complete searches for *Fortune* 500 Companies, I have particular success with privately held companies—companies where a smaller firm can serve a broad range of needs. These are generally also companies where the smaller amount of total business available doesn't attract larger competitors.

Knowing the business and the potential clients and their businesses gave me the pieces I needed to achieve initial success and to continue to build a successful business.

SUN TZU THROUGH OTHER EYES:

"I don't throw darts at a board. I bet on sure things. Read Sun-Tzu, *The Art of War*. Every battle is won before it is ever fought."

—*Wall Street,* 1989 movie,
spoken by the character Gordon Gecko

"Been reading that book you told me about. You know, *The Art of War* by Sun Tzu. I mean here's this guy, a Chinese general, wrote this thing 2,400 years ago, and most of it still applies today! Balk the enemy's power. Force him to reveal himself. You know most of the guys that I know, they read Prince Machiavelli and I had Carmela go and get the Cliff Notes once and he's okay. But this book is much better about strategy."

—*The Sopranos,* TV series, spoken by the character Tony Soprano

"We must not belittle the saying in the book of Sun Tzu, the great military expert of ancient China, 'Know your enemy and know yourself and you can fight a thousand battles without disaster.'"

—General Vo Nguyen Giap, Commander in Chief of the People's
Army of Vietnam (North Vietnam) during the Vietnam War

"I've read the Chinese classic *The Art of War* written by Sun Tzu. Sun Tzu has been studied for hundreds of years. He continues to give inspiration to soldiers and politicians. So every American soldier in the army knows of his works. We require our soldiers to read it."

—Former Chairman of the Joint Chiefs of Staff Colin Powell

"Mr. Benioff quotes *The Art of War,* written by the ancient Chinese general Sun Tzu and a favorite read with many managers. 'In the military more is not better, you don't have to be large to win battles, and that's true in the technology industry as well.'"

—BBC Article quoting Salesforce.com CEO Mark Benioff

Outline of Key Concepts

Thoroughly Assess Conditions

Sun Tzu	Business
Moral Influence	Vision and Mission
Weather	Outside Influences
Terrain	Marketplace
Command	Leadership
Doctrine	Core Beliefs

Compare Attributes

- Which side is managed by those who have established meaningful objectives (with a high moral value)?
- Which people have the most ability?
- Which side can take the best advantage of current conditions?
- Which side has better discipline?
- Which side is stronger?
- Which side is better trained?
- Which side is better motivated?

Look for Strategic Turns

- Go beyond ordinary rules.
- Search for advantages.
- Find favorable strategic conditions.
- Examine the situation thoroughly.
- Do the unexpected.
- Build your own strengths.
- Continuously analyze the strengths and weaknesses of the opposition.

CHAPTER TWO: WAGING WAR

Marshal Adequate Resources

When resources are depleted and cannot be replenished, the organization goes bankrupt.

Make Time Your Ally

- Victory is the main objective.
- "While we have heard of stupid haste, we have not yet seen a clever operation that was prolonged."
- When the operation takes too long:
    Resources may be depleted.
    Weapons are blunted.
    Morale is depressed.
    Your opponents will take advantage of your distress.
- "What is valued is a quick victory, not prolonged operations."
- Those who do not understand the dangers do not understand how to make advantageous use of resources.
- Those that are adept do not require additional resources.

Everyone Must Profit from Victories

- When others go out of business, profit by acquiring their physical and human resources.
- Win by acquiring competitors and making good use of their people in the new organization structure.

This is called winning and becoming stronger.

Know Your Craft

The objective is winning, not spending time. The leaders who truly understand their business control the battle and achieve victory.

CHAPTER THREE: ATTACK BY STRATAGEM

Win Without Fighting

- Consider making opponents into allies.
- The best victories are those that can be won without conflict:
    First, attack strategy. This is the best approach.

Next, disrupt alliances.
If these do not work, consider fighting, but do not attack strengths.

Strength Against Weakness—Always

- The greater your strength compared to your opponent, the greater the chances for winning.
- If resources are equally matched, fight only if you have special abilities.
- The small cannot defeat the large, nor the weak the strong, nor the few the many.

Beware of "High-Level Dumb"

- Those who are not at the scene of action and do not know what is going on should not give orders.
- Each business should be managed by those with extensive experience in that business.
- Rules established at corporate headquarters should not necessarily apply to every distant operation.

Obey Fundamental Principles

- Know when you can be on the offensive and when you must take the defensive.
- Where you have superiority, use one strategy; where you are inferior, use another.
- Seek those actions that have high unity of purpose.
- Be prepared for contingencies.
- Headquarters should be careful of interfering.

CHAPTER FOUR : DISPOSITION OF MILITARY STRENGTH

Be Invincible

- What you do determines whether you are defeated.
- What your opponent does determines whether you can win.
- Because you know how to win does not mean that you will win.
- Secure your defenses; however, you must take the offensive to win.
- When you have insufficient strength, you must defend.
- When you have an overabundance of strength, attack.
- Tactics used in the defense are different from those used in the attack.

Attain Strategic Superiority

- The best strategy is to win without fighting. This often requires looking beyond the obvious to find the unusual.
- Achieving victory while avoiding conflict requires skillful insight and forethought in planning.
- Your strategy must be so good that:
  You cannot possibly be defeated.
  It takes advantage of every opportunity.
- The side that wins will be the side for which victory was certain before the battle began.
- Those destined to defeat fight in the hope of winning.
- The winning leader understands the moral law and strictly adheres to method and discipline.

Use Information to Focus Resources

- Understand your opponent's position and strength.
- Consider where you can have relative superiority.
- Plan to attain overwhelming superiority at a decisive point.
- Build the force of momentum.

CHAPTER FIVE: USE OF ENERGY

Build a Sound Organization Structure

- Control is a matter of organization and communications.
- Use the same fundamental principles regardless of size.

Apply Extraordinary Force

- That which directly confronts your opponent is the normal or direct force.
- That which strikes at his weakest areas is the extraordinary or indirect force.
- Keep your opponent confused concerning routes of attack.
- Plan the impact of the very strong against the very weak.
- Use the normal force to engage, the extraordinary to win.
- The combination of the normal and the extraordinary is an endless circle of direct and indirect engagements.

Coordinate Momentum and Timing
- Your actions must have the energy of momentum and take place at the most advantageous time.
- Whether there is order amidst apparent confusion depends upon organization.
- When planning creates favorable circumstances, you have the advantage of high morale.
- Whether you are weak or strong depends on all of the arrangements you have made.
- All of the strength will come from the people alone; the leader must create the situation for victory.
- People must be selected for a task on the basis of their ability—not on nepotism or favoritism.
- The energy created is the combined energy of all people and all resources.

CHAPTER SIX: WEAKNESS AND STRENGTH

Take the Initiative
- Those that occupy the field of battle first and await their enemy are at ease. Those who come later to the scene and rush into the fight are weary.
- Those skilled in war bring the enemy to the battlefield and are not brought there by their opponent.
- You either offer some advantage to get the enemy to your battlefield or do things to prevent the enemy from coming.

Plan Surprise
Consider these actions to surprise and harass your enemy:
- When at ease, make your opponent weary.
- When well fed, starve your opponent.
- When at rest, make your opponent move.
- Appear where your opponent must hasten.
- Move swiftly where not expected.

Attack	**Defense**
To take what you attack, attack the unprotected.	To hold what you defend, defend a place that will not be attacked.
Against those skilled in attack, an enemy does not know where to defend.	Against the experts in defense, the enemy does not know where to attack.
Those whose advance is irresistible plunge into their enemy's weak positions.	Those who in withdrawal cannot be pursued move so swiftly they cannot be overtaken.

Gain Relative Superiority

- If I am able to determine my enemy's dispositions while I conceal my own, then:
    I can concentrate and my enemy must divide.
    I can use my strength to attack a fraction of my enemy's strength; therefore, I will be superior.
- The enemy must not know where I intend to give battle.
    If my opponent does not, she must prepare in many places.
    If my opponent prepares in many places, those I fight in any one place will be few.
- One who has few must prepare against the enemy.
- One who has many makes the enemy prepare against her.

Seek Knowledge

- Those who know where and when the battle will be fought can marshal all of their resources to the right place.
- If one knows neither where nor when the battle will be fought, his forces will be unable to aid each other.
- Victory can be created (even if the enemy is more numerous, we can prevent him from engaging).
- Determine the enemy's plans and we know whether our strategy will work.
- Stir the enemy up and determine his patterns.
- Probe to learn strengths and weaknesses.

Be Flexible

- While you shape your opponent, do not let her discern your shape.
- Strategies do not change with the times.

- Just as water rushes down and shapes its course according to the ground, avoid strengths and strike weaknesses—work out victory in relation to your foe.
- As water has no constant form, there are no constant conditions.
- Because the situation is constantly changing, you must continually modify your tactics.

CHAPTER SEVEN: MANEUVERING

Maneuver to Gain the Advantage
- Make the devious route the most direct.
- Turn misfortune into advantage.
- Use deception.
- Make changes to confuse your opponent.

Achieve the Critical Mass
- Consider these issues carefully:
  Know those with whom you enter into alliances.
  Know the situation and use the help of others who have had the same experience.
- Gather all your resources and you will be too late. Advance without enough resources and you may lose them all.
- Divide the profits of your ventures.

Deceive Your Competitor
The purpose of deception is not to keep your opponent from arriving at the objective; rather, the purpose is to make her arrive too late to be of any harm.

Develop Effective Internal Communications
- Have a method for clear communication.
- Do not use the same communications for every situation.

Gain the Mental Advantage
- Preserve your resources for the main effort.
- Do not fight battles you cannot win.
- Adapt quickly to changes in the circumstances.

- Do not do that which your opponent wishes you to do—if for no other reason than he so wishes.
- Do not press a desperate opponent too hard.

CHAPTER EIGHT: VARIATION OF TACTICS

Consider Tactical Options
- Understand the mission, gather resources, and concentrate the offensive.
  Do not tarry where an advantage cannot be gained.
  Form alliances where necessary.
  When limited options are available, resort to strategy.
  Fight when there is no alternative.
- There are:
  Business opportunities we should not follow
  Competitors we should not attack
  Accounts we should not do business with
  Positions we cannot win
  Instructions we should not follow
- Advantages alone are not enough.
- Whether at the advantage or the disadvantage, always keep in mind what you would do in the opposite state.
- To gain the advantage, consider what the opponent would do to gain the advantage.
- Use attorneys and others to make trouble for your opponent.

Prepare Adequate Defenses
Do not rely on the opponent not attacking, but rather expect that he will and prepare accordingly.

Avoid the Faults of Leadership
- Bravery can lead to recklessness and destruction.
- Being overly cautious leads to cowardice and defeat.
- Anger leads to temper with vulnerability to insults.
- Delicate honor leads to sensitivity and bad reactions.
- Worry leads to oversolicitude and blunders.

CHAPTER NINE: ON THE MARCH

Occupy Strong Natural Positions
- Keep close to resources that fortify your strengths.
- Position yourself so that your opponent has a disadvantage.
- Try to keep your opponent from taking advantage of natural strengths that might be available to her.

Always Seek the High Ground
- Be concerned for the health of your people.
- Do not occupy imperiled positions; let your opponent do that.
- Fight downhill.

Make an Estimate of the Situation
- Watch for signs that tell you what your opponent is doing.
- Study the actions and mood of your opponent's people.
- If your opponent is giving lavish incentives, he is near the end of his resources.
- Treat every opponent as a threat—be careful not to underestimate.

Discipline Can Build Allegiance
- Treat your people with humanity.
- Instill a sense of discipline.
- Trust and confidence must be mutual—otherwise, it does not exist.

CHAPTER TEN: TERRAIN

Know Your Battlefield
- Arrive early and get the best positions.
- In questionable markets, let your competitor enter first to determine whether opportunity exists.
- Develop strengths in narrow niche markets.
- Attack only those segments weakly defended.
- Vigorously defend profitable and unique markets.
- Distant markets can be difficult to serve.

Obey the Laws of Leadership

- If the leader attacks strength, she will lose.
- When instructions are clear, everyone will act with confidence; if unclear, every action will be disorganized.
- When leaders are unable to accurately estimate the overall situation, the result will be bankruptcy.

Fight Only the Battles You Can Win

- Use the strength of natural positions.
- Know how to estimate the strength of your opponent.
- Be shrewd in calculating dangers and difficulties.
- It is not enough to know what you should do. You must also put into practice that which you know.
- Do not act in your own self-interest, but rather in the best interests of your people and organization.
- Retreat from bad situations.

Know Yourself; Know Your Opponent

- Knowing yourself is not enough; you must also know where your opponent is strong and where he is weak.
- Your chances of victory are greatly enhanced when you attack weakness and avoid strength.

CHAPTER ELEVEN: THE NINE VARIETIES OF GROUND

Choose a Favorable Battleground

Each opportunity must consider the situation:

- Do not fight internally.
- Do not attack or defend where you cannot have the advantage.
- When you can neither advance nor retreat, concentrate on protecting yourself.
- When progress is difficult, keep on the offensive.
- When outnumbered, resort to strategy.
- Fight courageously when desperate.

Shape Your Opponent's Strategy

- Do what you lawfully can to disrupt your opponent's internal communications, cooperation, morale, and cohesion.

- Advance when you can gain an advantage; stay where you are when no advantage can be gained.
- Seize the initiative so you can keep your opponent on the defensive.
- Speed is essential. Move rapidly and miss no opportunity.

Make Victory the Only Option

- The more successful you are, the greater will be the morale and the more certain will be your future success.
- Devise winning plans and actively solicit new resources.
- Make certain the consequences of failure of the organization are understood.
- Fighting for survival assures unity and develops its own strength.
- The skillful tactician accepts the attack in one area and strikes back in another.

Plan Coordinated Efforts

- Foster actions that encourage internal cooperation.
- Do not rely on the physical to win; victory comes only from a tenacious team united in purpose.
- Set high standards for performance.
- Utilize the strength of natural positions.

Press the Attack

- Keep people united.
- Manage calmly.
- Be just and maintain order.
- Understand there are things not to say publicly because this would aid the opponent.
- Keep the opponent confused.
- Make sure that everyone is motivated to succeed and avoid failure.

Learn Winning Ways

- The leader is knowledgeable concerning:
    The plans of allies and competitors
    The fields of conflict
    People who can win
- Always shape your strategy to the situation.

CHAPTER TWELVE: ATTACK BY FIRE

Be Disruptive and Intrusive
- Use the most decisive weapons available to attack.
- Disrupt your opponent and intrude into that disruption.
- Be an entrepreneur in developing your offensive.

Consolidate Your Gains
- Reinforce successful efforts and exploit opportunities that arise.
- Encourage and reward the spirit of enterprise.
- Lay plans carefully and take action.

Exercise Restraint
- Attack only when you see an advantage.
- Do not expend energy simply to gratify your own interests.
- Do not attack to satisfy your own anger.
- Losses cannot be recovered.
- Be prudent and do not take rash actions.

CHAPTER THIRTEEN: EMPLOYMENT OF SECRET AGENTS

Invest in Intelligence Resources
- A major effort requires major resources. Expect opposition from those who are burdened by this.
- Do not ignore the rewards and honors that will help motivate people. Small sums can bring big results.
- Allocate the resources necessary to gain the information you will need.
- The cost of unnecessarily prolonged operations will be much greater than the cost of information that will help to win quickly.

Establish an Active Intelligence System
- Good information is critical to success. This information must come from those who know the situation.
- Beware of those who can only give opinions. This baseless information will mislead.
- Develop a network that can provide information.
- Send out people whose only purpose is to gather information.
- Invite in all who can be a source of information.

- Look for those special people who may have the most information about the situation.
- Get all the information that can be lawfully gleaned from people you interview and from those you then employ.

Practice Counterintelligence

- Do not do things that can give information to your opponent.
- Beware the visitor who gratuitously gives you information concerning your opponent. She may also be providing information about you to the other side.

NOTES

Chapter One

1. Kenichi Ohmae, *The Borderless World* (Harper Business, 1990), pp.73–74.
2. Tim Carvell, "Prime-Time Player," *Fortune*, March 2, 1998, pp. 134–144.
3. General Bill Creech, *The Five Pillars of TQM* (New York, Plume/Penguin, 1994).
4. *Financial Times*, October 3, 2009.

Chapter Two

1. Captain H. M. Johnstone, *The Foundations of Strategy* (London, George Allen & Unwin, 1914).
2. *Inc.*, October, 2009.
3. "The 100 Best," *Industry Week*, August 17, 1998, pp. 37–74.
4. Gerald A. Michaelson, *Winning the Marketing War* (Knoxville, Tennessee, Pressmark International, 1987), pp. 80–81.
5. Shawn Tully, "Merrill Lynch Takes Over," *Fortune*, April 27, 1998, pp. 138–144.
6. Eric O'Keefe, "Gannon Luck," *Polo Magazine*, July/August 1998, pp. 65–68.

Chapter Three

1. B. H. Liddell Hart, *Strategy* (New York, Praeger Publishers, 1967), p. 339.
2. Michaelson, *Winning the Marketing War*, pp. 135–136.
3. Norman Dixon, *On the Psychology of Military Incompetence* (London, Jonathan Cape, 1976).
4. Michaelson, *Winning the Marketing War*, p. 30.

Chapter Four

1. David Ogilvy, *Ogilvy on Advertising* (Vintage Books, 1983), p. 47.
2. Chris Mcrae, "Chain of Thought," *Marketing Business*, April 1996, pp. 34–35.
3. Anne Faircloth, "The Best Retailer You've Never Heard Of," *Fortune*, March 16, 1998, pp. 110–112.
4. Ram Charan, "The Rules Have Changed," *Fortune*, March 16, 1998, p. 159.

Chapter Five

1. Michaelson, *Winning the Marketing War*, p. 13.
2. Gina Imperato, "Harley Shifts Gears," *Fast Company*, 1998.
3. Gerald Sentell, *Creating Change-Capable Cultures* (Knoxville, Tennessee, Pressmark International, 1998), p. 155.

Chapter Six

1. Ronald B. Lieber, "Stop Your Whining," *Fortune*, October 13, 1997, pp. SB3–6.
2. Michaelson, *Winning the Marketing War*, p. 94.

Chapter Seven

1. Michaelson, *Winning the Marketing War*, pp. 92–98.
2. Michaelson, *Winning the Marketing War*, p. 5.
3. Rucci, Kirn, and Quinn, "The Employee-Customer-Profit Chain at Sears," *Harvard Business Review*, January/February 1998, pp. 83–97.

Chapter Eight

1. Matt Goldberg, "Microsoft Knows How to Operate—Fast," *Fast Company*, April/May 1998.
2. Brig. Gen. Robert L. Stewart, "New Technology: Another Way to Get Oats to the Horses?" *Army*, January 1995, pp. 23–27.
3. Donald V. Fites, "Make Your Dealer Your Partners," *Harvard Business Review*, March/April 1996, pp. 84–95.
4. Anna Muoio, "The Truth Is, the Truth Hurts, " *Fast Company*, April/May 1998, p. 93.

Chapter Nine

1. Lesley Hazleton, "Jeff Bezos," *SUCCESS*, July 1998, pp. 58–60.
2. Herman Cain, "Leadership Is Common Sense" (book bonus), *SUCCESS*, January/February 1997, pp. 41–48.

Chapter Ten

1. Michaelson, *Winning the Marketing War*, pp. 124–128.
2. Michaelson, *Winning the Marketing War*, p. 67.

Chapter Eleven

1. Frank Rose, "The Eisner School of Business," *Fortune*, July 6, 1998, pp. 29–30.
2. Bartlett & Ghoshal, *The Individualized Corporation* (Harper Business, 1997).
3. Ardant du Picq, *Battle Studies* (Harrisburg, Pennsylvania, The Military Service Publishing Co., 1958).
4. Eisenhardt, Kahwajy, and Bourgeois, "How Management Teams Can Have a Good Fight," *Harvard Business Review*, July/August 1997, pp. 77–85.

Chapter Twelve

1. Ohmae, *The Borderless World*, p. 28.

Chapter Thirteen

1. Pascale, Millemann, and Gioja, "Changing the Way We Change," *Harvard Business Review*, November/December 1997, pp. 127–139.
2. Michaelson, *Winning the Marketing War*, p. 34.

Bibliography

von Clausewitz, Carl. *On War,* Princeton, NJ: Princeton University Press, 1976.

Creech, Bill, General. *The Five Pillars of TQM.* New York: Plume/Penguin, 1994.

Dixon, Norman. *On the Psychology of Military Incompetence.* London: Jonathan Cape, 1976.

du Picq, Ardant, Colonel. *Battle Studies.* Harrisburg, Pennsylvania: The Military Science Publishing Co., 1958.

Fuller, J. F. C. *The Conduct of War.* London: Eyre & Spottiswoode, 1961.

Fuller, J. F. C. *Generalship: Its Diseases and Their Cure.* Out of print.

Halberstam, David. *The Reckoning.* New York: William Morrow and Company, 1986.

Hart, B. H. Liddel. *Great Captains Unveiled.* London: Blackwood, 1927.

Hart, B. H. Liddel. *Strategy.* New York, Praeger Publishers, 1967.

Henderson, G. F. R., Colonel. *The Science of War.* London: Longmans, Green and Co., 1905.

Johnstone, Henry Melville, Captain. *The Foundations of Strategy.* London: George, Allen & Unwin, 1914.

Kets de Vries, Manfred F. R. *Life and Death in the Executive Fast Lane: Essays on Irrational Organizations and Their Leaders.* San Francisco: Jossey-Bass Publishers, 1995.

Levinson, Harry. *The Exceptional Executive.* Out of print.

Mahan, A. T. *The Influence of Sea Power upon History.* New York: Hill and Wang, 1957.

Mao Tse-tung. *Mao Tse-tung: On Guerrilla War,* 1937. (From Heinl, Jr., Robert Debs. *Dictionary of Military and Naval Quotations.* Annapolis, Maryland: United States Naval Institute, 1966.)

Michaelson, Gerald A. *Winning the Marketing War.* Knoxville, Tennessee: Pressmark International, 1987.

Sentell, Gerald. *Creating Change-Capable Cultures.* Knoxville, Tennessee: Pressmark international, 1998.

Translator's Bibliography

(Includes only books containing a complete translation of *The Art of War* used for research for this book.)

Ames, Roger. *Sun Tzu: The Art of Warfare*. New York: Ballantine Books, 1993. Includes analysis, complete text, and "five hitherto unknown chapters."

Bruya, Brian. *Sun Zi Speaks* (Sun Zi is the Chinese spelling and more clipped phonic of Sun Tzu). New York: Anchor Books, 1966. This book is illustrated by Tsai Chih Chung, with cartoon-like drawings accompanying each sentence.

Chien-sein Ko. *The Art of War by Sun Tzu in Chinese and English*. Publisher unknown, 1973. Out of print.

Clavell, James. *The Art of War Sun Tzu*. New York: Delta by Dell, 1988. Written by a novelist with his interpretations of the ideograms, which lack the combative interpretations of military authors.

Cleary, Thomas. *The Art of War Sun Tzu*. Boston & London: Shamballa, 1988. Original translation plus extensive commentary by eleven interpreters.

Giles, Lionel. *Sun Tzu on the Art of War*. Singapore: Graham Brash Ltd., 1988. Includes extensive annotations for every sentence.

Griffith, Samuel B., General. *Sun Tzu The Art of War*. London: Oxford, New York: Oxford Press, 1963. Extensive commentary throughout.

Hanzhang, Tao, General, *Sun Tzu's Art of War*. New York, Sterling Pub., 1987.

Krause, Donald G. *The Art of War for Executives*. New York: Berkeley, 1995. Lots of interpretive commentary but may not include entire translation.

Phillips, Major Thomas R. Numerous translations, including *The Art of War*. Westport, Connecticut: Greenwood Press, 1940.

Sadler, A. L. *Three Military Classics of China* (including Sun Tzu). Sydney: Australasian medical, 1944. Probably out of print.

Sawyer, Ralph D. *Sun Tzu Art of War*. Boulder, Colorado: Westview Press, 1994. Original text plus extensive commentary. The Complete Art of War Sun Tzu, Sun Pin, 1996.

Tai Mien-leng. *The Art of War*. Publisher unknown. Out of print.

Tang Zi-chang. *Principles of Conflict*. T. C. Press. Out of print.

Wing, R. L. *The Art of Strategy*. New York: Doubleday.

Zhang Huimin. *Sun Zi, The Art of War*. Publisher unknown. Includes extensive text in Asian languages and succinct commentary.

Index

About the Authors

Gerald A. Michaelson was the author of many business books, including the classic *The Art of War for Managers* and others in the Sun Tzu series including *Strategies for Success*, *Sun Tzu for Sales*, and *Sun Tzu for Marketing*. His titles also include *Building Bridges to Customers* and *Winning the Marketing War: A Field Manual*.

Gerald Michaelson spent more than twenty-five years growing sales for Magnavox/Phillips in sales, marketing, and ultimately as a corporate vice president, using the strategic concepts set forth in this book. As a writer and consultant, he was internationally recognized. He was a featured speaker at an international symposium on Sun Tzu's the Art of War in Beijing, China, and returned to conduct management seminars for the Chinese government utilizing Sun Tzu's strategic concepts. His articles appeared in leading periodicals of his time including *Success* magazine, *World Executive's Digest*, *Traveler* in Asia, *Executive Edge*, and *Sales and Marketing Management*. He also wrote a weekly column for newspapers in the Scripps Howard network. He was a member of the Board of Directors of the American Marketing Association and of fast-growing companies. He appeared on every continent speaking on his insights from Sun Tzu.

Michaelson's diverse experiences as a Korean War Veteran, a *Fortune* 500 executive, a consultant, writer, and author gave him the broad background that culminated in the classic *Sun Tzu: The Art of War for Managers*. He passed away in 2004.

Steven Michaelson is Gerald's son. Accomplished in his own right, he has led a diverse set of large and small companies in a variety of leadership roles. His twenty-five years of business experience includes brand management at Procter & Gamble, retail leadership as a senior vice president of highly honored retailer Wegmans, CEO of New York's FreshDirect, and Chief Marketing Officer of a *Fortune* 100 company.

Steven Michaelson is the author of *Sun Tzu: The Art of Execution* and previously coauthored several of the Sun Tzu titles with his father. He has spoken at industry conferences for small businesses, information technology, retailing, and consumer packaged goods across the country, and written for a variety of publications.

E-mail: *swmichaelson@juno.com*

Website: *www.stevemichaelson.com*

Authors' pages on Amazon